OPENING LINES
poetry past and present

Opening Lines is OCR's new collection of poems, originally published before and after 1914, designed to meet the requirements of the National Curriculum Programme of Study and of the QCA Subject Criteria for GCSE English and English Literature (2002).

Opening Lines is an optional prescribed poetry text for OCR GCSE in English (specification 1900) and for OCR GCSE in English Literature (specification 1901), for examinations between June 2003 and January 2008 onwards. For full details of all examination requirements, please refer to the specification booklets, available from OCR, 1 Hills Road, Cambridge CB1 2EU or www.ocr.org.uk. You will also find further details about the poets on our website. Further support for study of the poems in *Opening Lines* is provided in *Working with Opening Worlds and Opening Lines*, published by Heinemann (ISBN 0435150979).

Using *Opening Lines* with the OCR specifications

OCR GCSE English (1900)

Coursework

For coursework in GCSE English Unit 4: Reading and Writing, poems in *Opening Lines* may be studied as appropriate to the requirements of the specification:

Poetry Pre-1914	Poetry Post-1914
Any poems in Part 1 by writers from the National Curriculum list of 'major poets published before 1914'. These poets are indicated by **NC** in the list of contents on pages 7, 21, 33, 45.	All poems in Part 2 are considered to be by 'major poets published after 1914'. Any of the poems in the four sections in Part 2 may therefore be used in coursework for English.

Examinations

Opening Lines is the prescribed poetry text for GCSE English Unit 3: Reading and Writing (the examination alternative to Unit 4, coursework).

In each examination session:
* two pre-1914 and two post-1914 sections in this collection are set for study
* candidates will be required to answer on *one section only*.

For examination in June 2003, January and June 2004, January and June 2005, January 2006	For examination in June 2006, January and June 2007, January 2008 onwards
(Candidates answer on one section only)	(Candidates answer on one section only)
Pre-1914	**Pre-1914**
Section A: Men and Women (page 7)	Section C: War (page 33)
Section B: Time and Change (page 21)	Section D: Town and Country (page 45)
Post-1914	**Post-1914**
Section E: Generations (page 59)	Section G: How It Looks From Here (page 87)
Section F: The 1914–18 War (i) (page 75)	Section H: The 1914–18 War (ii) (page 101)

OCR GCSE English Literature (1901)

Coursework

For coursework in GCSE English Literature Unit 3 or Unit 7, any of the poems in *Opening Lines* may be studied as appropriate to the requirements of the specification and of the Scheme (A or B) being followed.

Examinations

Opening Lines is an optional prescribed poetry text for examinations in GCSE English Literature.

In each examination session:
- two sections in this collection are prescribed for study, as appropriate to the Unit (pre-1914 or post-1914) and the Scheme (A or B) being followed
- candidates will be required to answer *on one of the prescribed sections only*
- Unit 4 (Scheme A) and Unit 8 (Scheme B) are examination alternatives to coursework.

For examination in June 2003, January and June 2004, January and June 2005, January 2006		For examination in June 2006, January and June 2007, January 2008 onwards	
Scheme A	**Scheme B**	**Scheme A**	**Scheme B**
Unit 2: Poetry and Prose Post-1914	**Unit 6: Poetry and Prose Pre-1914**	**Unit 2: Poetry and Prose Post-1914**	**Unit 6: Poetry and Prose Pre-1914**
Section E: Generations (page 59)	Section A: Men and Women (page 7)	Section G: How It Looks From Here (page 87)	Section C: War (page 33)
Section F: The 1914–18 War (i) (page 75)	Section B: Time and Change (page 21)	Section H: The 1914–18 War (ii) (page 101)	Section D: Town and Country (page 45)
Unit 4: Pre-1914 Texts	**Unit 8: Post-1914 Texts**	**Unit 4: Pre-1914 Texts**	**Unit 8: Post-1914 Texts**
Section A: Men and Women (page 7)	Section E: Generations (page 59)	Section C: War (page 33)	Section G: How It Looks From Here (page 87)
Section B: Time and Change (page 21)	Section F: The 1914–18 War (i) (page 75)	Section D: Town and Country (page 45)	Section H: The 1914–18 War (ii) (page 101)

'Overlap' between requirements

English and English Literature

Candidates who are entering Units in the same session for both subjects may, if they wish, study the *same selection of poems for both English and English Literature*. The same poems may be studied for coursework in both subjects, and common pieces of work may be submitted in the folder; or the same prescribed selection of poems may be studied for examinations in each subject. (Separate question papers will be set for each subject.)

Coursework and examinations

In both English and English Literature, candidates have the option to enter either for coursework or for an alternative examination. Additionally, if they wish, candidates may 'double bank' and enter for *both* coursework *and* examination.

If they wish to 'double bank' coursework and examination in this way, either in English or in English Literature, candidates are advised to study for coursework the *same selection of poems as that prescribed for the examination* they intend to take.

OCR (Oxford Cambridge and RSA Examinations)
1 Hills Road, Cambridge CB1 2EU

© Oxford Cambridge and RSA Examinations 2002

First published 2002
Reprinted 2002, 2003, 2004, 2005, 2008

ISBN: 978 0 435150 94 5

Produced by Heinemann Educational

Designed and typeset by Jackie Hill at 320 Design

Illustrated by John Holder pp.13, 22, 27, 41, 48; David Hopkins pp.15, 27, 30, 37, 43, 49, 55, 71, 72, 79, 90, 104, 107;
Rachael Wilkinson p.108.

Cover design by hicksdesign

Cover photographs: A soldier and his bride: Mary Evans Picture Library; WWI soldiers around a camp fire: Hulton Getty; Red autumn leaves on the ground: Getty Images/Image Bank; Mother and daughter: Getty Images/Image Bank

Printed and bound in Great Britain by Scotprint

Acknowledgements

The Publishers wish to thank the following who have kindly granted permission for the use of copyright material:
'The Listeners' by Walter de la Mare, from *The Complete Poems of Walter de la Mare*, 1969. Reprinted with permission of the Literary Trustees of Walter de la Mare and the Society of Authors as their representative; 'Into my heart. . .' and 'On Wenlock Edge. . .' by A. E. Housman, reprinted with permission of The Society of Authors as the Literary Representative of The Estate of A. E. Housman; 'Vitaï Lampada' by Henry Newbolt, from *Selected Poems of Henry Newbolt*, published by Hodder & Stoughton, 1981. Reprinted with the kind permission of Peter Newbolt; 'The Hyaenas' and 'The Way Through the Woods' by Rudyard Kipling, reprinted with permission of A. P. Watt Limited on behalf of The National Trust for Places of Historical Interest or Natural Beauty; 'The Lake Isle of Innisfree' by W. B. Yeats, reprinted with permission of A. P. Watt Limited on behalf of Michael B. Yeats; 'You're' and 'Mirror' by Sylvia Plath, from *Collected Poems*, published by Faber and Faber Limited. Reprinted with permission of Faber and Faber Limited; 'Baby-sitting' and 'Clocks' by Gillian Clarke, from *Collected Poems*, published by Carcanet Press Limited. Reprinted with permission of Carcanet Press Limited; 'To Edwin, at Eight Months' and 'West Pathway' by Steve Ellis, from *West Pathway*, published by Bloodaxe Books, 1993. Copyright © Steve Ellis 1993. Reprinted with the kind permission of the author; 'Growing Up' by U. A. Fanthorpe, from *Voices Off*, published by Peterloo Poets, 1984. Reprinted with the kind permission of the author; 'To Carry The Child' and 'Oh Grateful Colours, Bright Looks!' by Stevie Smith, reprinted with the kind permission of The Estate of James MacGibbon; 'I Remember, I Remember' and 'Wedding-Wind' by Philip Larkin, first published in *Less Deceived* by Marvell Press; 'Anseo' by Paul Muldoon, from *New Selected Poems*, published by Faber and Faber Limited. Reprinted with permission of Faber and Faber Limited; 'A Short Film' by Ted Hughes, from *Birthday Letters*, published by Faber and Faber Limited. Reprinted with permission of Faber and Faber Limited; 'Poem' by Simon Armitage, copyright © Simon Armitage. Reprinted with permission of David Godwin Associates; 'Follower' by Seamus Heaney, from *Opened Ground*, published by Faber and Faber Limited. Reprinted with permission of Faber and Faber Limited; 'Imitations' by Dannie Abse, copyright © Dannie Abse, published by Hutchinson. Reprinted with permission of Peters Fraser & Dunlop on behalf of Dannie Abse; 'Long Distance II' by Tony Harrison, published in *Selected Poems*, published by Penguin. Copyright © Tony Harrison. Reprinted with permission of Gordon Dickerson on behalf of Tony Harrison; 'The Flowers' and 'The Hare' by Selima Hill, from *Trembling Hearts in the Bodies of Dogs: New and Selected Poems*, published by Bloodaxe Books, 1994. Reprinted with permission of Bloodaxe Books; 'The Tune The Old Cow Died Of' by Norman Nicholson, from *Collected Poems*, published by Faber and Faber Limited. Reprinted with permission of David Higham Associates Limited; 'War Girls' by Jessie Pope, from *Simple Rhymes for Stirring Times*, published in 1916 by Arthur C. Pearson. Reprinted with permission of The Hamlyn Group; 'Base Details', 'The Dug-Out', 'Lamentations' and 'The Hero' by Siegfried Sassoon. Copyright © Siegfried Sassoon. Reprinted with kind permission of George Sassoon via Barbara Levy Literary Agency; 'Breakfast' by W. W. Gibson, from *Collected Poems* published by Macmillan. Reprinted with permission of the publishers; 'Easter Monday' by Eleanor Farjeon, from *Book of Days* published by Oxford University Press. Reprinted with permission of David Higham Associates Limited; 'There will come soft rains. . .' by Sara Teasdale, from *The Collected Poems of Sara Teasdale*. Published by New York: Macmillan, 1937. Reprinted with the permission of Simon & Schuster Inc.; 'A Consumer's Report' and 'Mort aux Chats' by Peter Porter. Copyright © Peter Porter. Reprinted with the kind permission of the author; 'The Cat and The Sea' by R. S. Thomas, from *R. S. Thomas Selected Poems 1946-1968*, published by Bloodaxe Books 1986. Reprinted with permission of Bloodaxe Books; 'Rat, O Rat' by Christopher Logue, from *Selected Poems*, published by Faber and Faber Limited. Reprinted with permission of Faber and Faber Limited; 'In Your Mind' by Carol Ann Duffy, from *The Other Country*, published by Anvil Press Poetry in 1990. Copyright © Carol Ann Duffy 1990. Reprinted with permission of the publishers; 'Judging Distances' by Henry Reed, from *Henry Reed: Collected Poems* edited by Jon Stallworthy, published by Oxford University Press, 1991. Reprinted with permission of Oxford University Press; 'Things' by Fleur Adcock, from *Poems 1960-2000*, published by Bloodaxe Books, 2000. Reprinted with permission of Bloodaxe Books; 'Bedfellows' by Don Paterson, from *Nil Nil*, published by Faber and Faber Limited. Reprinted with permission of Faber and Faber Limited; 'Defying Gravity' by Roger McGough, from *Defying Gravity*, published by Penguin Books. Copyright © Roger McGough. Reprinted with permission of Peters Fraser & Dunlop on behalf of Roger McGough; 'I Am a Cameraman' by Douglas Dunn, from *Selected Poems*, published by Faber and Faber Limited. Reprinted with permission of Faber and Faber Limited; 'Engineers' Corner' by Wendy Cope from *Making Cocoa for Kingsley Amis*, published by Faber and Faber Limited. Reprinted with permission of Faber and Faber Limited; 'Sometimes' by Sheenagh Pugh, from *Selected Poems*, published by Seren Books. Copyright © Sheenagh Pugh 1990. Reprinted with permission of the publishers; 'Joining the Colours' by Katherine Tynan, from *Flower of Youth*, published in 1918 by Sidgwick and Jackson; 'The Deserter' by Winifred M. Letts, from *Hallowe'en and Poems of the War*, published by John Murray. Reprinted with permission of John Murray (Publishers) Limited; 'The Falling Leaves' by Margaret Postgate Cole, reprinted with permission of David Higham Associates Limited; 'Perhaps -' by Vera Brittain, reprinted with the kind permission of her literary executors, Mark Bostridge and Rebecca Williams.

Whilst every effort has been made to locate the owners of copyright, in some cases this has been unsuccessful. The publishers apologise for any omission of original sources and will be pleased to make the necessary arrangements at the first opportunity.

Poetry Pre-1914

PART 1

Men and Women

SECTION A

Pre-1914

For examination in June 2003, January and June 2004, January and June 2005, January 2006

The Sun Rising

Busy old fool, unruly Sun,
    Why dost thou thus,
Through windows and through curtains call on us?
Must to thy motions lovers' seasons run?
5   Saucy pedantic wretch, go chide
      Late school-boys, and sour 'prentices,
  Go tell court-huntsmen that the King will ride,
  Call country ants to harvest offices;
Love, all alike, no season knows, nor clime,
10 Nor hours, days, months, which are the rags of time.

Thy beams, so reverend and strong
    Why shouldst thou think?
I could eclipse and cloud them with a wink,
But that I would not lose her sight so long:
15   If her eyes have not blinded thine,
      Look, and tomorrow late tell me,
  Whether both th'Indias of spice and mine
  Be where thou left'st them, or lie here with me.
Ask for those kings whom thou saw'st yesterday,
20 And thou shalt hear, 'All here in one bed lay'.

She's all States, and all Princes, I;
    Nothing else is.
Princes do but play us; compared to this,
All honour's mimic; all wealth alchemy.
25   Thou, Sun, art half as happy as we,
      In that the world's contracted thus;
  Thine age asks ease, and since thy duties be
  To warm the world, that's done in warming us.
Shine here to us, and thou art everywhere;
30 This bed thy centre is, these walls thy sphere.

John Donne (1572–1631)

Upon Julia's Clothes

Whenas in silks my Julia goes,
Then, then, methinks, how sweetly flows
That liquefaction of her clothes!

Next, when I cast mine eyes and see
5 That brave vibration each way free,
Oh, how that glittering taketh me!

Robert Herrick (1591–1674)

To His Coy Mistress

Had we but world enough, and time,
This coyness, Lady, were no crime.
We would sit down, and think which way
To walk, and pass our long love's day.
5   Thou by the Indian Ganges' side
Shouldst rubies find: I by the tide
Of Humber would complain. I would
Love you ten years before the flood:
And you should, if you please, refuse
10 Till the conversion of the Jews.
My vegetable love should grow
Vaster than empires, and more slow.
An hundred years should go to praise
Thine eyes, and on thy forehead gaze.
15 Two hundred to adore each breast:
But thirty thousand to the rest.
An age at least to every part,
And the last age should show your heart:
For, Lady, you deserve this state;
20 Nor would I love at lower rate.
        But at my back I always hear
Time's wingèd chariot hurrying near:
And yonder all before us lie
Deserts of vast eternity.
25 Thy beauty shall no more be found;
Nor, in thy marble vault, shall sound
My echoing song: then worms shall try
That long-preserved virginity:
And your quaint honour turn to dust;
30 And into ashes all my lust.
The grave's a fine and private place,
But none, I think, do there embrace.
        Now, therefore, while the youthful hue
Sits on thy skin like morning dew,
35 And while thy willing soul transpires
At every pore with instant fires,
Now let us sport us while we may;
And now, like amorous birds of prey,
Rather at once our time devour,
40 Than languish in his slow-chapped power.
Let us roll all our strength, and all
Our sweetness, up into one ball:
And tear our pleasures with rough strife,
Thorough the iron gates of life.
45 Thus, though we cannot make our sun
Stand still, yet we will make him run.

Andrew Marvell (1621–78)

The Ruined Maid

'O 'Melia, my dear, this does everything crown!
Who could have supposed I should meet you in Town?
And whence such fair garments, such prosperi-ty?' –
'O didn't you know I'd been ruined?' said she.

5   – 'You left us in tatters, without shoes or socks,
Tired of digging potatoes, and spudding up docks;
And now you've gay bracelets and bright feathers three!' –
'Yes: that's how we dress when we're ruined,' said she.

  – 'At home in the barton you said "thee" and "thou",
10   And "thik oon", and "theäs oon", and "t'other"; but now
Your talking quite fits 'ee for high compa-ny!' –
'Some polish is gained with one's ruin,' said she.

  – 'Your hands were like paws then, your face blue and bleak
But now I'm bewitched by your delicate cheek,
15   And your little gloves fit as on any la-dy!' –
'We never do work when we're ruined,' said she.

  – 'You used to call home-life a hag-ridden dream,
And you'd sigh, and you'd sock; but at present you seem
To know not of megrims or melancho-ly!' –
20   'True. One's pretty lively when ruined,' said she.

  – 'I wish I had feathers, a fine sweeping gown,
And a delicate face, and could strut about Town!' –
'My dear – a raw country girl, such as you be,
Cannot quite expect that. You ain't ruined,' said she.

Thomas Hardy (1840–1928)

Sonnet

How do I love thee? Let me count the ways.
    I love thee to the depth and breadth and height
    My soul can reach, when feeling out of sight
For the ends of Being and ideal Grace.
5   I love thee to the level of every day's
    Most quiet need, by sun and candlelight.
    I love thee freely, as men strive for Right;
I love thee purely, as they turn from Praise.
I love thee with the passion put to use
10   In my old griefs, and with my childhood's faith.
I love thee with a love I seemed to lose
    With my lost saints – I love thee with the breath,
Smiles, tears, of all my life! – and, if God choose,
    I shall but love thee better after death.

Elizabeth Barrett Browning (1806 – 61)

Sonnet 138

When my love swears that she is made of truth,
I do believe her, though I know she lies,
That she might think me some untutor'd youth,
Unlearned in the world's false subtleties.
5   Thus vainly thinking that she thinks me young,
Although she knows my days are past the best,
Simply I credit her false-speaking tongue:
On both sides thus is simple truth supprest.
But wherefore says she not she is unjust?
10 And wherefore say not I that I am old?
O! love's best habit is in seeming trust,
And age in love loves not to have years told:
    Therefore I lie with her, and she with me,
    And in our faults by lies we flatter'd be.

William Shakespeare (1564 – 1616)

The Unequal Fetters

Could we stop the time that's flying
    Or recall it when 'tis past,
Put far off the day of dying
    Or make youth for ever last,
5   To love would then be worth our cost.

But since we must lose those graces
    Which at first your hearts have won
And you seek for in new faces
    When our spring of life is done,
10   It would but urge our ruin on.

Free as Nature's first intention
    Was to make us, I'll be found,
Nor by subtle Man's invention
    Yield to be in fetters bound
15   By one that walks a freer round.

Marriage does but slightly tie men
    Whilst close prisoners we remain,
They the larger slaves of Hymen
    Still are begging love again
20   At the full length of all their chain.

Anne Finch (1661–1720)

A Woman Is a Worthy Thing

I am light as any roe
To praise women where that I go.

To unpraise women it were shame,
For a woman was Thy dame;
5   Our blessed lady bereth the name
    Of all women where that they go.

A woman is a worthy thing:
They do the wash and do the wring;
'Lullay, lullay' she doth thee sing;
10   And yet she hath but care and wo.

A woman is a worthy wight:
She serveth a man both day and night;
Therto she putteth all her might;
    And yet she hath but care and wo.

Anon. (medieval)

A Scherzo
A Shy Person's Wishes

With the wasp at the innermost heart of a peach,
On a sunny wall out of tip-toe reach,
With the trout in the darkest summer pool,
With the fern-seed clinging behind its cool
5 Smooth frond, in the chink of an aged tree,
In the woodbine's horn with the drunken bee,
With the mouse in its nest in a furrow old,
With the chrysalis wrapped in its gauzy fold;
With things that are hidden, and safe, and bold,
10 With things that are timid, and shy, and free,
Wishing to be;
With the nut in its shell, with the seed in its pod,
With the corn as it sprouts in the kindly clod,
Far down where the secret of beauty shows
15 In the bulb of the tulip, before it blows;
With things that are rooted, and firm, and deep,
Quiet to lie, and dreamless to sleep;
With things that are chainless, and tameless, and proud,
With the fire in the jagged thunder-cloud,
20 With the wind in its sleep, with the wind in its waking,
With the drops that go to the rainbow's making,
Wishing to be with the light leaves shaking,
Or stones in some desolate highway breaking;
Far up on the hills, where no foot surprises
25 The dew as it falls, or the dust as it rises;
To be couched with the beast in its torrid lair,
Or drifting on ice with the polar bear,
With the weaver at work at his quiet loom;
Anywhere, anywhere, out of this room!

Dora Greenwell (1821–82)

Faithless Sally Brown

Young Ben he was a nice young man,
    A carpenter by trade;
And he fell in love with Sally Brown,
    That was a lady's maid.

5   But as they fetch'd a walk one day,
    They met a press-gang crew;
And Sally she did faint away,
    Whilst Ben he was brought to.

The Boatswain swore with wicked words,
10   Enough to shock a saint,
That though she did seem in a fit,
    'Twas nothing but a feint.

'Come girl,' said he, 'hold up your head,
    He'll be as good as me;
15   For when your swain is in our boat,
    A boatswain he will be.'

So when they'd made their game of her,
    And taken off her elf,
She roused, and found she only was
20   A coming to herself.

'And is he gone, and is he gone?'
    She cried and wept outright:
'Then I will to the water side,
    And see him out of sight.'

25   A waterman came up to her, –
    'Now, young woman,' said he
'If you weep on so, you will make
    Eye-water in the sea.'

'Alas! they've taken my beau Ben
30   To sail with old Benbow;'
And her woe began to run afresh,
    As if she'd said Gee woe!

Says he, 'They've only taken him
    To the Tender ship, you see;'
35   'The Tender-ship,' cried Sally Brown,
    'What a hard-ship that must be!'

'O! would I were a mermaid now,
    For then I'd follow him;
But Oh! – I'm not a fish-woman,
40   And so I cannot swim.'

'Alas! I was not born beneath
    The virgin and the scales,
So I must curse my cruel stars,
    And walk about in Wales.'

45 Now Ben had sail'd to many a place
    That's underneath the world;
But in two years the ship came home,
    And all her sails were furl'd.

But when he call'd on Sally Brown,
50   To see how she went on,
He found she'd got another Ben,
    Whose Christian-name was John.

'O Sally Brown, O Sally Brown,
    How could you serve me so?
55 I've met with many a breeze before,
    But never such a blow.'

Then reading on his 'bacco box
    He heav'd a bitter sigh,
And then began to eye his pipe,
60   And then to pipe his eye.

And then he tried to sing 'All's Well,'
    But could not though he tried;
His head was turn'd, and so he chew'd
    His pigtail till he died.

65 His death, which happen'd in his berth,
    At forty-odd befell:
They went and told the sexton, and
    The sexton toll'd the bell.

Thomas Hood (1799–1845)

They flee from me . . .

They flee from me that sometime did me seek
With naked foot stalking in my chamber.
I have seen them gentle, tame, and meek
That now are wild and do not remember
5   That sometime they put themself in danger
To take bread at my hand; and now they range
Busily seeking with a continual change.

Thanked be fortune it hath been otherwise
Twenty times better, but once in special,
10   In thin array after a pleasant guise,
When her loose gown from her shoulders did fall
And she me caught in her arms long and small,
Therewithal sweetly did me kiss
And softly said, 'Dear heart, how like you this?'

15   It was no dream: I lay broad waking.
But all is turned thorough my gentleness
Into a strange fashion of forsaking.
And I have leave to go of her goodness
And she also to use newfangleness.
20   But since that I so kindly am served
I would fain know what she hath deserved.

Sir Thomas Wyatt (1503– 42)

Since there's no help . . .

Since there's no help, come, let us kiss and part.
Nay, I have done; you get no more of me;
And I am glad, yea, glad with all my heart,
That thus so cleanly I myself can free.
5   Shake hands for ever; cancel all our vows;
And when we meet at any time again,
Be it not seen in either of our brows
That we one jot of former love retain.
Now at the last gasp of Love's latest breath,
10   When, his pulse failing, Passion speechless lies,
When Faith is kneeling by his bed of death,
And Innocence is closing up his eyes;

Now, if thou would'st, when all have given him over,
From death to life thou might'st him yet recover.

Michael Drayton (1563–1631)

On the Departure Platform

We kissed at the barrier; and passing through
She left me, and moment by moment got
Smaller and smaller, until to my view
    She was but a spot;

5   A wee white spot of muslin fluff
That down the diminishing platform bore
Through hustling crowds of gentle and rough
    To the carriage door.

Under the lamplight's fitful glowers,
10   Behind dark groups from far and near,
Whose interests were apart from ours,
    She would disappear,

Then show again, till I ceased to see
That flexible form, that nebulous white;
15   And she who was more than my life to me
    Had vanished quite. . . .

We have penned new plans since that fair fond day,
And in season she will appear again –
Perhaps in the same soft white array –
20   But never as then!

– 'And why, young man, must eternally fly
A joy you'll repeat, if you love her well?'
– O friend, nought happens twice thus; why,
    I cannot tell!

Thomas Hardy (1840–1928)

The Sick Rose

O Rose, thou art sick!
The invisible worm
That flies in the night,
In the howling storm,

5   Has found out thy bed
Of crimson joy:
And his dark secret love
Does thy life destroy.

William Blake (1757–1827)

Remember

Remember me when I am gone away,
    Gone far away into the silent land;
    When you can no more hold me by the hand,
Nor I half turn to go yet turning stay.
5   Remember me when no more day by day
    You tell me of our future that you planned:

    Only remember me; you understand
It will be late then to counsel or to pray.
Yet if you should forget me for a while
10   And afterwards remember, do not grieve:
    For if the darkness and corruption leave
    A vestige of the thoughts that once I had,
Better by far you should forget and smile
    Than that you should remember and be sad.

Christina Rossetti (1830–93)

In the Mile End Road

How like her! But 'tis she herself,
    Comes up the crowded street,
How little did I think, the morn,
My only love to meet?

5   Whose else that motion and that mien?
    Whose else that airy tread?
For one strange moment I forgot
My only love was dead.

Amy Levy (1861–89)

Time and Change

SECTION B

Pre-1914

For examination in June 2003, January and June 2004, January and June 2005, January 2006

I Remember, I Remember

I remember, I remember,
The house where I was born,
The little window where the sun
Came peeping in at morn;
5 He never came a wink too soon
Nor brought too long a day,
But now, I often wish the night
Had borne my breath away!

I remember, I remember,
10 The roses, red and white,
The violets, and the lily-cups,
Those flowers made of light!
The lilacs where the robin built,
And where my brother set
15 The laburnum on his birthday, –
The tree is living yet!

I remember, I remember,
Where I was used to swing,
And thought the air must rush as fresh
20 To swallows on the wing;
My spirit flew in feathers then,
That is so heavy now,
And summer pools could hardly cool
The fever on my brow!

25 I remember, I remember,
The fir trees dark and high;
I used to think their slender tops
Were close against the sky:
It was a childish ignorance,
30 But now 'tis little joy
To know I'm further off from heav'n
Than when I was a boy.

Thomas Hood (1799–1845)

The Listeners

'Is there anybody there?' said the Traveller,
    Knocking on the moonlit door;
And his horse in the silence champed the grasses
    Of the forest's ferny floor:
5   And a bird flew up out of the turret,
    Above the Traveller's head:
And he smote upon the door again a second time;
    'Is there anybody there?' he said.
But no one descended to the Traveller;
10   No head from the leaf-fringed sill
Leaned over and looked into his grey eyes,
    Where he stood perplexed and still.
But only a host of phantom listeners
    That dwelt in the lone house then
15   Stood listening in the quiet of the moonlight
    To that voice from the world of men:
Stood thronging the faint moonbeams on the dark stair,
    That goes down to the empty hall,
Hearkening in an air stirred and shaken
20   By the lonely Traveller's call.
And he felt in his heart their strangeness,
    Their stillness answering his cry,
While his horse moved, cropping the dark turf,
    'Neath the starred and leafy sky;
25   For he suddenly smote on the door, even
    Louder, and lifted his head:–
'Tell them I came, and no one answered,
    That I kept my word,' he said.
Never the least stir made the listeners,
30   Though every word he spake
Fell echoing through the shadowiness of the still house
    From the one man left awake:
Ay, they heard his foot upon the stirrup,
    And the sound of iron on stone,
35   And how the silence surged softly backward,
    When the plunging hoofs were gone.

Walter de la Mare (1873–1956)

Ozymandias

I met a traveller from an antique land
Who said: Two vast and trunkless legs of stone
Stand in the desert ... Near them, on the sand,
Half sunk, a shattered visage lies, whose frown,
5   And wrinkled lip, and sneer of cold command,
Tell that its sculptor well those passions read
Which yet survive, stamped on these lifeless things,
The hand that mocked them, and the heart that fed:
And on the pedestal these words appear:
10 'My name is Ozymandias, king of kings:
Look on my works, ye Mighty, and despair!'
Nothing beside remains. Round the decay
Of that colossal wreck, boundless and bare
The lone and level sands stretch far away.

Percy Bysshe Shelley (1792–1822)

Into my heart . . .

Into my heart an air that kills
   From yon far country blows:
What are those blue remembered hills,
   What spires, what farms are those?

5   That is the land of lost content,
    I see it shining plain,
The happy highways where I went
   And cannot come again.

A. E. Housman (1859–1936)

To the Virgins, to Make Much of Time

Gather ye rosebuds while ye may,
   Old Time is still a-flying:
And this same flower that smiles to-day
   To-morrow will be dying.

5   The glorious lamp of heaven, the sun,
   The higher he's a-getting,
The sooner will his race be run,
   And nearer he's to setting.

That age is best which is the first,
10   When youth and blood are warmer;
But being spent, the worse, and worst
   Times still succeed the former.

Then be not coy, but use your time,
   And while ye may, go marry:
15 For having lost but once your prime,
   You may for ever tarry.

Robert Herrick (1591–1674)

Spring and Fall

To a young child

Margaret, are you grieving
Over Goldengrove unleaving?
Leaves, like the things of man, you
With your fresh thoughts care for, can you?
5 Ah! as the heart grows older
It will come to such sights colder
By and by, nor spare a sigh
Though worlds of wanwood leafmeal lie;
And yet you will weep and know why,
10 Now no matter, child, the name:
Sorrow's springs are the same.
Nor mouth had, no nor mind, expressed
What heart heard of, ghost guessed:
It is the blight man was born for,
15 It is Margaret you mourn for.

Gerard Manley Hopkins (1844–89)

Woak Hill

When sycamore leaves wer a-spreaden,
  Green-ruddy, in hedges,
Bezide the red doust o' the ridges,
  A-dried at Woak Hill;

5 I packed up my goods all a-sheenen
  Wi' long years o' handlen
On dousty red wheels ov a waggon,
  To ride at Woak Hill.

The brown thatchen ruf o' the dwellen,
10 I then wer a-leäven,
Had shelter'd the sleek head o' Meäry,
  My bride at Woak Hill.

But now vor zome years, her light voot-vall
  'S a-lost vrom the vlooren.
15 Too soon vor my jay an' my childern,
  She died at Woak Hill.

But still I do think that, in soul,
  She do hover about us;
To ho vor her motherless childern,
20 Her pride at Woak Hill.

Zoo – lest she should tell me hereafter
  I stole off 'ithout her,
An' left her, uncall'd at house-ridden,
  To bide at Woak Hill –

25 I call'd her so fondly, wi' lippens
  All soundless to others,
An' took her wi' aïr-reachen hand,
  To my zide at Woak Hill.

On the road I did look round, a-talken
30 To light at my shoulder,
An' then led her in at the door-way,
  Miles wide vrom Woak Hill.

An' that's why vo'k thought, vor a season,
  My mind wer a-wandren
35 Wi' sorrow, when I wer so sorely
  A-tried at Woak Hill.

But no; that my Meäry mid never
  Behold herzelf slighted,
I wanted to think that I guided
40 My guide vrom Woak Hill.

William Barnes (1801–86)

The Darkling Thrush

I leant upon a coppice gate
　　When Frost was spectre-gray,
And Winter's dregs made desolate
　　The weakening eye of day.
5　The tangled bine-stems scored the sky
　　Like strings of broken lyres,
And all mankind that haunted nigh
　　Had sought their household fires.

The land's sharp features seemed to be
10　The Century's corpse outleant,
His crypt the cloudy canopy,
　　The wind his death-lament.
The ancient pulse of germ and birth
　　Was shrunken hard and dry,
15　And every spirit upon earth
　　Seemed fervourless as I.

At once a voice arose among
　　The bleak twigs overhead
In a full-hearted evensong
20　Of joy illimited;
An aged thrush, frail, gaunt, and small,
　　In blast-beruffled plume,
Had chosen thus to fling his soul
　　Upon the growing gloom.

25　So little cause for carolings
　　Of such ecstatic sound
Was written on terrestrial things
　　Afar or nigh around,
That I could think there trembled through
30　His happy good-night air
Some blessed Hope, whereof he knew
　　And I was unaware.

Thomas Hardy (1840–1928)

The Latest Decalogue

Thou shalt have one God only; who
Would be at the expense of two?
No graven images may be
Worshipped, except the currency:
5   Swear not at all; for, for thy curse
Thine enemy is none the worse:
At church on Sunday to attend
Will serve to keep the world thy friend:
Honour thy parents; that is, all
10 From whom advancement may befall;
Thou shalt not kill; but need'st not strive
Officiously to keep alive:
Do not adultery commit;
Advantage rarely comes of it:
15 Thou shalt not steal; an empty feat,
When it's so lucrative to cheat:
Bear not false witness; let the lie
Have time on its own wings to fly:
Thou shalt not covet, but tradition
20 Approves all forms of competition.

Arthur Hugh Clough (1819–61)

A Song

Lying is an occupation,
   Used by all who mean to rise;
Politicians owe their station,
   But to well concerted lies.

5 These to lovers give assistance,
   To ensnare the fair-one's heart;
And the virgin's best resistance
   Yields to this commanding art.

Study this superior science,
10   Would you rise in Church or State;
Bid to Truth a bold defiance,
   'Tis the practice of the great.

Laetitia Pilkington (1712–50)

On the Times

Now is Ingland all in fight;
Much peple of consciens light;
Many knightes and litel of might;
Many lawes and litel right;
5   Many actes of parlament
And few kept with tru entent
Litel charite and fain to plese;
Many a gallant penylese;
And many a wonderful disgising
10   By prudent and misadvising;
Grete countenance and smalle wages;
Many gentilemen and few pages;
Wide gownes and large sleves;
Wel besene and strong theves;
15   Much bost of their clothes,
But wel I wot they lake none othes.

Anon. (c.1450)

A Poison Tree

I was angry with my friend:
I told my wrath, my wrath did end.
I was angry with my foe:
I told it not, my wrath did grow.

5   And I water'd it in fears,
Night and morning with my tears;
And I sunned it with smiles,
And with soft deceitful wiles.

And it grew both day and night,
10   Till it bore an apple bright;
And my foe beheld it shine,
And he knew that it was mine,

And into my garden stole
When the night had veil'd the pole:
15   In the morning glad I see
My foe outstretch'd beneath the tree.

William Blake (1757–1827)

The Poison Flower

The poison flower that in my garden grew
Killed all the other flowers beside.
They withered off and died,
Because their fiery foe sucked up the dew.

5   When the sun shone, the poison flower breathed cold
And spread a chilly mist of dull disgrace.
They could not see his face,
Roses and lilies languished and grew old.

Wherefore I tore that flower up by the root,
10   And flung it on the rubbish heap to fade
Amid the havoc that itself had made.
I did not leave one shoot.

Fair is my garden as it once was fair.
Lilies and roses reign.
15   They drink the dew, they see the sun again;
But I rejoice no longer, walking there.

Mary Coleridge (1861–1907)

The Gray Folk

The house, with blind unhappy face,
    Stands lonely in the last year's corn,
    And in the grayness of the morn
The gray folk come about the place.

5   By many pathways, gliding gray
    They come past meadow, wood, and wold,
    Come by the farm and by the fold
From the green fields of yesterday.

Past lock and chain and bolt and bar
10   They press, to stand about my bed,
    And like the faces of the dead
I know their hidden faces are.

They will not leave me in the day
    And when night falls they will not go,
15   Because I silenced, long ago,
The only voice they will obey.

Edith Nesbit (1858–1924)

Dreams

Here we are all, by day; by night we're hurled
By dreams, each one, into a several world.

Robert Herrick (1591–1674)

Death the Leveller

The glories of our blood and state
    Are shadows, not substantial things;
There is no armour against Fate;
    Death lays his icy hand on kings:
5   Sceptre and Crown
        Must tumble down,
And in the dust be equal made
With the poor crookèd scythe and spade.

Some men with swords may reap the field,
10   And plant fresh laurels where they kill:
But their strong nerves at last must yield;
    They tame but one another still:
        Early or late
        They stoop to fate,
15 And must give up their murmuring breath
When they, pale captives, creep to death.

The garlands wither on your brow;
    Then boast no more your mighty deeds!
Upon Death's purple altar now
20   See where the victor-victim bleeds.
        Your heads must come
        To the cold tomb:
Only the actions of the just
Smell sweet and blossom in their dust.

James Shirley (1596–1666)

War
SECTION C

Pre-1914

For examination in June 2006, January and June 2007, January 2008 onwards

To Lucasta,
Going to the Wars

Tell me not, sweet, I am unkind,
 That from the nunnery
Of thy chaste breast and quiet mind
 To war and arms I fly.

5 True, a new mistress now I chase,
 The first foe in the field;
And with a stronger faith embrace
 A sword, a horse, a shield.

Yet this inconstancy is such
10 As you too shall adore;
I could not love thee, dear, so much,
 Loved I not honour more.

Richard Lovelace (1618–?1657/8)

The Volunteer

Here lies a clerk who half his life had spent
Toiling at ledgers in a city grey,
Thinking that so his days would drift away
With no lance broken in life's tournament.
5 Yet ever 'twixt the books and his bright eyes
The gleaming eagles of the legions came,
And horsemen, charging under phantom skies,
Went thundering past beneath the oriflamme.

And now those waiting dreams are satisfied;
10 From twilight to the halls of dawn he went;
His lance is broken; but he lies content
With that high hour, in which he lived and died.
And falling thus he wants no recompense,
Who found his battle in the last resort;
15 Nor need he any hearse to bear him hence,
Who goes to join the men of Agincourt.

Herbert Asquith (1852–1928)

Vitaï Lampada

There's a breathless hush in the Close to-night –
    Ten to make and the match to win –
A bumping pitch and a blinding light,
    An hour to play and the last man in.
5 And it's not for the sake of a ribboned coat,
    Or the selfish hope of a season's fame,
But his Captain's hand on his shoulder smote –
    'Play up! play up! and play the game!'

The sand of the desert is sodden red, –
10   Red with the wreck of a square that broke; –
The Gatling's jammed and the Colonel dead,
    And the regiment blind with dust and smoke.
The river of death has brimmed his banks,
    And England's far, and Honour a name,
15 But the voice of a schoolboy rallies the ranks:
    'Play up! play up! and play the game!'

This is the word that year by year,
    While in her place the School is set,
Every one of her sons must hear,
20   And none that hears it dare forget.
This they all with a joyful mind
    Bear through life like a torch in flame,
And falling fling to the host behind –
    'Play up! play up! and play the game!'

Henry Newbolt (1862–1938)

On Lieutenant Eyre's Narrative of the Disasters of Cabul

A sorry tale of sorry plans,
Which this conclusion grants,
That Afghan clans had all the *Khans*
And we had all the can'ts.

Thomas Hood (1799–1845)

The Charge of the Light Brigade

I

Half a league, half a league,
    Half a league onward,
All in the valley of Death
    Rode the six hundred.
5 'Forward, the Light Brigade!
Charge for the guns!' he said:
Into the valley of Death
    Rode the six hundred.

II

'Forward, the Light Brigade!'
10 Was there a man dismayed?
Not though the soldier knew
    Some one had blundered:
Their's not to make reply,
Their's not to reason why,
15 Their's but to do and die:
Into the valley of Death
    Rode the six hundred.

III

Cannon to right of them,
Cannon to left of them,
20 Cannon in front of them
    Volleyed and thundered;
Stormed at with shot and shell,
Boldly they rode and well,
Into the jaws of Death,
25 Into the mouth of Hell
    Rode the six hundred.

IV

Flashed all their sabres bare,
Flashed as they turned in air
Sabring the gunners there,
30 Charging an army, while
    All the world wondered:
Plunged in the battery-smoke
Right through the line they broke;
Cossack and Russian
35 Reeled from the sabre-stroke
    Shattered and sundered.
Then they rode back, but not,
    Not the six hundred.

V

Cannon to right of them,
40 Cannon to left of them,
Cannon behind them
    Volleyed and thundered;
Stormed at with shot and shell,
While horse and hero fell,
45 They that had fought so well
Came through the jaws of Death,
Back from the mouth of Hell,
All that was left of them,
    Left of six hundred.

VI

When can their glory fade?
50 O the wild charge they made!
    All the world wondered.
Honour the charge they made!
Honour the Light Brigade,
55   Noble six hundred!

Alfred, Lord Tennyson (1809–92)

The Destruction of Sennacherib

The Assyrian came down like the wolf on the fold,
And his cohorts were gleaming in purple and gold;
And the sheen of their spears was like stars on the sea,
When the blue wave rolls nightly on deep Galilee.

5 Like the leaves of the forest when Summer is green,
That host with their banners at sunset were seen:
Like the leaves of the forest when Autumn hath blown,
That host on the morrow lay wither'd and strown.

For the Angel of Death spread his wings on the blast,
10 And breathed in the face of the foe as he pass'd;
And the eyes of the sleepers wax'd deadly and chill,
And their hearts but once heaved, and for ever grew still!

And there lay the steed with his nostril all wide,
But through it there roll'd not the breath of his pride;
15 And the foam of his gasping lay white on the turf,
And cold as the spray of the rock-beating surf.

And there lay the rider distorted and pale,
With the dew on his brow, and the rust on his mail;
And the tents were all silent, the banners alone,
20 The lances uplifted, the trumpet unblown.

And the widows of Ashur are loud in their wail,
And the idols are broken in the temple of Baal;
And the might of the Gentile, unsmote by the sword,
Hath melted like snow in the glance of the Lord!

Lord Byron (1788–1824)

After Blenheim

I

It was a summer evening,
   Old Kaspar's work was done,
And he before his cottage door
   Was sitting in the sun:
5 And by him sported on the green
His little grandchild Wilhelmine.

II

She saw her brother Peterkin
   Roll something large and round
Which he beside the rivulet
10   In playing there had found:
He came to ask what he had found
That was so large, and smooth, and round.

III

Old Kaspar took it from the boy
   Who stood expectant by;
15 And then the old man shook his head,
   And with a natural sigh
''Tis some poor fellow's skull,' said he,
'Who fell in the great victory.

IV

'I find them in the garden,
20   For there's many here about;
And often when I go to plough
   The ploughshare turns them out.
For many thousand men,' said he,
'Were slain in that great victory.'

V

25 'Now tell us what 'twas all about,'
   Young Peterkin, he cries;
And little Wilhelmine looks up
   With wonder-waiting eyes;
'Now tell us all about the war,
30 And what they fought each other for.'

VI

'It was the English,' Kaspar cried,
   'Who put the French to rout;
But what they fought each other for
   I could not well make out.
35 But everybody said,' quoth he,
'That 'twas a famous victory.

VII

'My father lived at Blenheim then,
   Yon little stream hard by;
They burnt his dwelling to the ground,
40   And he was forced to fly:
So with his wife and child he fled
Nor had he where to rest his head.

VIII

'With fire and sword the country round
   Was wasted far and wide,
45 And many a childing mother then,
   And newborn baby died:
But things like that, you know, must be
At every famous victory.

IX

'They say it was a shocking sight
50   After the field was won;
For many thousand bodies here
   Lay rotting in the sun:
But things like that, you know, must be
After a famous victory.

X

55 'Great praise the Duke of Marlboro' won
   And our good Prince Eugene.'
'Why, 'twas a very wicked thing!'
   Said little Wilhelmine;
'Nay . . . nay . . . my little girl,' quoth he,
60 'It was a famous victory.

XI

'And everybody praised the Duke
   Who this great fight did win.'
'But what good came of it at last?'
   Quoth little Peterkin.
65 'Why that I cannot tell,' said he,
'But 'twas a famous victory.'

Robert Southey (1774–1843)

Come up from the fields father . . .

Come up from the fields father, here's a letter from our Pete,
And come to the front door mother, here's a letter from thy dear son.

Lo, 'tis autumn,
Lo, where the trees, deeper green, yellower and redder,
5   Cool and sweeten Ohio's villages with leaves fluttering in the moderate wind,

Where apples ripe in the orchards hang and grapes on the trellis'd vines,
(Smell you the smell of the grapes on the vines?
Smell you the buckwheat where the bees were lately buzzing?)
Above all, lo, the sky so calm, so transparent after the rain, and with wondrous clouds,
10   Below too, all calm, all vital and beautiful, and the farm prospers well.

Down in the fields all prospers well,
But now from the fields come father, come at the daughter's call,
And come to the entry mother, to the front door come right away.

Fast as she can she hurries, something ominous, her steps trembling,
15   She does not tarry to smooth her hair nor adjust her cap.

Open the envelope quickly,
O this is not our son's writing, yet his name is sign'd,
O a strange hand writes for our son, O stricken mother's soul!

All swims before her eyes, flashes with black, she catches the main words only,
20   Sentences broken, *gunshot wound in the breast, cavalry skirmish, taken to hospital,*
At present low, but will soon be better.

Ah now the single figure to me,
Amid all teeming and wealthy Ohio with all its cities and farms,
Sickly white in the face and dull in the head, very faint,
25   By the jamb of a door leans.

Grieve not so, dear mother, (the just-grown daughter speaks through her sobs,
The little sisters huddle around speechless and dismay'd,)
See, dearest mother, the letter says Pete will soon be better.

Alas poor boy, he will never be better, (nor may-be needs to be better, that brave and simple soul,)
30   While they stand at home at the door he is dead already,
The only son is dead.

But the mother needs to be better,
She with thin form presently drest in black,
By day her meals untouch'd, then by night fitfully sleeping, often waking,
35   In the midnight waking, weeping, longing with one deep longing,
O that she might withdraw unnoticed, silent from life escape and withdraw,
To follow, to seek, to be with her dear dead son.

Walt Whitman (1819–92)

Tommy's Dead

You may give over plough, boys,
You may take the gear to the stead;
All the sweat o' your brow, boys,
Will never get beer and bread.
5   The seed's waste, I know, boys;
There's not a blade will grow, boys;
'Tis cropped out, I trow, boys,
And Tommy's dead.

Send the colt to the fair, boys –
10   He's going blind, as I said,
My old eyes can't bear, boys,
To see him in the shed;
The cow's dry and spare, boys,
She's neither here nor there, boys,
15   I doubt she's badly bred;
Stop the mill to-morn, boys,
There'll be no more corn, boys,
Neither white nor red;
There's no sign of grass, boys,
20   You may sell the goat and the ass, boys,
The land's not what it was, boys,
And the beasts must be fed;
You may turn Peg away, boys,
You may pay off old Ned,
25   We've had a dull day, boys,
And Tommy's dead.

Outside and in,
The ground is cold to my tread,
The hills are wizen and thin,
30   The sky is shrivelled and shred;
The hedges down by the loan
I can count them bone by bone,
The leaves are open and spread.
But I see the teeth of the land,

35   And hands like a dead man's hand,
And the eyes of a dead man's head.
There's nothing but cinders and sand,
The rat and the mouse have fled,
And the summer's empty and cold;
40   Over valley and wold,
Wherever I turn my head,
There's a mildew and a mould;
The sun's going out overhead,
And I'm very old,
45   And Tommy's dead.

What are you about, boys?
The prayers are all said,
The fire's raked out, boys,
And Tommy's dead.

50   The stairs are too steep, boys,
You may carry me to the head,
The night's dark and deep, boys,
Your mother's long in bed;
'Tis time to go to sleep, boys,
55   And Tommy's dead.

Sydney Dobell (1824–74)

Song

We know where deepest lies the snow,
And where the frost-winds keenest blow,
    O'er every mountain's brow,
We long have known and learnt to bear
5   The wandering outlaw's toil and care,
But where we late were hunted, there
    Our foes are hunted now.

We have their princely homes, and they
To our wild haunts are chased away,
10   Dark woods, and desert caves.
And we can range from hill to hill,
And chase our vanquished victors still;
Small respite will they find until
    They slumber in their graves.

15 But I would rather be the hare
That crouching in its sheltered lair
    Must start at every sound;
That forced from cornfields waving wide
Is driven to seek the bare hillside,
20 Or in the tangled copse to hide,
    Than be the hunter's hound.

Anne Brontë (1820– 49)

The Hyaenas

After the burial-parties leave
    And the baffled kites have fled;
The wise hyaenas come out at eve
    To take account of our dead.

5 How he died and why he died
    Troubles them not a whit.
They snout the bushes and stones aside
    And dig till they come to it.

They are only resolute they shall eat
10   That they and their mates may thrive,
And they know the dead are safer meat
    Than the weakest thing alive.

(For a goat may butt, and a worm may sting,
    And a child will sometimes stand;
15 But a poor dead soldier of the King
    Can never lift a hand.)

They whoop and halloo and scatter the dirt
    Until their tushes white
Take good hold in the army shirt,
20   And tug the corpse to light,

And the pitiful face is shewn again
    For an instant ere they close;
But it is not discovered to living men –
    Only to God and to those

25 Who, being soulless, are free from shame,
    Whatever meat they may find.
Nor do they defile the dead man's name –
    That is reserved for his kind.

Rudyard Kipling (1865–1936)

The Man He Killed

'Had he and I but met
By some old ancient inn,
We should have sat us down to wet
Right many a nipperkin!

5   'But ranged as infantry,
And staring face to face,
I shot at him as he at me,
And killed him in his place.

'I shot him dead because –
10   Because he was my foe,
Just so: my foe of course he was;
That's clear enough; although

'He thought he'd 'list, perhaps,
Off-hand like – just as I –
15 Was out of work – had sold his traps –
No other reason why.

'Yes; quaint and curious war is!
You shoot a fellow down
You'd treat if met where any bar is,
20   Or help to half-a-crown.'

Thomas Hardy (1840–1928)

Ode, Written in the Beginning of the Year 1746

How sleep the brave, who sink to rest
By all their country's wishes blest!
When Spring, with dewy fingers cold,
Returns to deck their hallowed mould,
5   She there shall dress a sweeter sod
Than Fancy's feet have ever trod.

By fairy hands their knell is wrung,
By forms unseen their dirge is sung;
There Honour comes, a pilgrim grey,
10   To bless the turf that wraps their clay,
And Freedom shall awhile repair
To dwell a weeping hermit there!

William Collins (1721–59)

On the Idle Hill

On the idle hill of summer,
    Sleepy with the flow of streams,
Far I hear the steady drummer
    Drumming like a noise in dreams.

5   Far and near and low and louder
    On the roads of earth go by,
Dear to friends and food for powder,
    Soldiers marching, all to die.

East and west on fields forgotten
10   Bleach the bones of comrades slain,
Lovely lads and dead and rotten;
    None that go return again.

Far the calling bugles hollo,
    High the screaming fife replies,
15   Gay the files of scarlet follow:
    Woman bore me, I will rise.

A. E. Housman (1859–1936)

The Drum

I hate that drum's discordant sound,
Parading round, and round, and round:
To thoughtless youth it pleasure yields,
And lures from cities and from fields,
5   To sell their liberty for charms
Of tawdry lace, and glittering arms;
And when Ambition's voice commands,
To march, and fight, and fall, in foreign lands.

I hate that drum's discordant sound,
10   Parading round, and round, and round:
To me it talks of ravaged plains,
And burning towns, and ruined swains,
And mangled limbs, and dying groans,
And widows' tears, and orphans' moans;
15   And all that Misery's hand bestows,
To fill the catalogue of human woes.

John Scott (1783–1821)

Verses
Inviting Mrs. C — to Tea on a public
Fast-day During the American War

Dear Stella, 'mid the pious sorrow
Our monarch bids us feel to-morrow,
The ahs! and ohs! supremely triste,
The abstinence from beef, and whist;
5   Wisely ordained to please the Lord,
And force him whet our edgeless sword,
Till, shipping o'er the Atlantic rill,
We cut provincial throats at will;
'Midst all the penitence we feel
10 For merry sins, – 'midst all the zeal
For vengeance on the saucy foe,
Who lays our boasted legions low;
I wish, when sullen evening comes,
That you, to gild its falling glooms,
15 Would, without scruple cold, agree
Beneath these walls to sip your tea.
From the chaste, fragrant, Indian weed
Our sins no pampering juices feed;
And though the hours, with contrite faces,
20 May banish the ungodly aces,
And take of food a sparing bit,
They'll gluttonize on Stella's wit.

'Tea!' cries a Patriot, 'on that day
'Twere good you flung the drug away,
25 Rememb'ring 'twas the cruel source
Of sad distrust, and long divorce
'Twixt nations, which, combined, had hurled
Their conquering javelin round the world.

'O! Indian shrub, thy fragrant flowers
30 To England's weal had deadly powers,
When Despotism, with impious hand,
To venom turned thy essence bland,
To venom, subtle, foul and fell,
As steeped the dart of Isdabel!

35 'Have we forgot the dread libation
Which cost the life of half the nation?
When Boston, with indignant thought
Saw poison in the perfumed draught,
And caused her troubled bay to be
40 But one vast bowl, of bitter tea;
While Ate, chiefly bidden guest,
Came sternly to the fatal feast,
And mingled with its baneful flood
Brothers'! – children's! – parents' blood;
45 Dire as the banquet Atreus served,
When his own son Thyestes carved,
And Phoebus, shrinking from the sight,
Drew o'er his orb the pall of night.

'Tomorrow then, at least, refrain,
50 Nor quaff thy bleeding country's bane!
For O! reflect, poetic daughter,
'Twas hapless Britain's laurel-water'.

Anna Seward (1747–1809)

Town and Country

SECTION D

Pre-1914

For examination in June 2006, January and June 2007, January 2008 onwards

The Passionate Shepherd to His Love

Come live with me, and be my love,
And we will all the pleasures prove,
That valleys, groves, hills, and fields,
Woods, or steepy mountain yields.

5   And we will sit upon the rocks,
Seeing the shepherds feed their flocks,
By shallow rivers to whose falls
Melodious birds sing madrigals.

And I will make thee beds of roses,
10   And a thousand fragrant posies,
A cap of flowers, and a kirtle,
Embroidered all with leaves of myrtle;

A gown made of the finest wool,
Which from our pretty lambs we pull;
15   Fair linèd slippers for the cold,
With buckles of the purest gold;

A belt of straw and ivy buds,
With coral clasps and amber studs:
And if these pleasures may thee move,
20   Come live with me, and be my love.

The shepherds' swains shall dance and sing
For thy delight each May morning.
If these delights thy mind may move,
Then live with me, and be my love.

Christopher Marlowe (1564–93)

The Nymph's Reply to the Shepherd

If all the world and love were young,
And truth in every shepherd's tongue,
These pretty pleasures might me move
To live with thee and be thy love.

5   But Time drives flocks from field to fold,
When rivers rage and rocks grow cold;
And Philomel becometh dumb;
The rest complains of cares to come.

The flowers do fade, and wanton fields
10   To wayward Winter reckoning yields:
A honey tongue, a heart of gall,
Is fancy's spring, but sorrow's fall.

Thy gowns, thy shoes, thy beds of roses,
Thy cap, thy kirtle, and thy posies,
15   Soon break, soon wither, soon forgotten
In folly ripe, in reason rotten.

Thy belt of straw and ivy buds,
Thy coral clasps and amber studs –
All these in me no means can move
20   To come to thee and be thy love.

But could youth last, and love still breed;
Had joys no date, nor age no need;
Then these delights my mind might move
To live with thee and be thy love.

Sir Walter Ralegh (c.1554–1618)

To Autumn

Season of mists and mellow fruitfulness,
    Close bosom-friend of the maturing sun,
Conspiring with him how to load and bless
    With fruit the vines that round the thatch-eaves run;
5   To bend with apples the mossed cottage-trees,
    And fill all fruit with ripeness to the core;
       To swell the gourd, and plump the hazel shells
With a sweet kernel; to set budding more,
    And still more, later flowers for the bees,
10   Until they think warm days will never cease,
       For summer has o'erbrimmed their clammy cells.

Who hath not seen thee oft amid thy store?
    Sometimes whoever seeks abroad may find
Thee sitting careless on a granary floor,
15   Thy hair soft-lifted by the winnowing wind;
Or on a half-reaped furrow sound asleep,
    Drowsed with the fume of poppies, while thy hook
       Spares the next swath and all its twinèd flowers;
And sometimes like a gleaner thou dost keep
20   Steady thy laden head across a brook;
Or by a cider-press, with patient look,
       Thou watchest the last oozings hours by hours.

Where are the songs of spring? Aye, where are they?
    Think not of them, thou hast thy music too –
25   While barred clouds bloom the soft-dying day,
    And touch the stubble-plains with rosy hue;
Then in a wailful choir the small gnats mourn
    Among the river sallows, borne aloft
       Or sinking as the light wind lives or dies;
30   And full-grown lambs loud bleat from hilly bourn;
    Hedge-crickets sing; and now with treble soft
The red-breast whistles from a garden-croft;
       And gathering swallows twitter in the skies.

John Keats (1795–1821)

Beeny Cliff

March 1870–March 1913

I

O the opal and the sapphire of that wandering western sea,
And the woman riding high above with bright hair flapping free –
The woman whom I loved so, and who loyally loved me.

II

The pale mews plained below us, and the waves seemed far away
5 In a nether sky, engrossed in saying their ceaseless babbling say,
As we laughed light-heartedly aloft on that clear-sunned March day.

III

A little cloud then cloaked us, and there flew an irised rain,
And the Atlantic dyed its levels with a dull misfeatured stain,
And then the sun burst out again, and purples prinked the main.

IV

10 – Still in all its chasmal beauty bulks old Beeny to the sky,
And shall she and I not go there once again now March is nigh,
And the sweet things said in that March say anew there by and by?

V

What if still in chasmal beauty looms that wild weird western shore,
The woman now is – elsewhere – whom the ambling pony bore,
15 And nor knows nor cares for Beeny, and will laugh there nevermore.

Thomas Hardy (1840–1928)

The Eagle

He clasps the crag with crooked hands;
Close to the sun in lonely lands,
Ring'd with the azure world, he stands.

The wrinkled sea beneath him crawls;
5 He watches from his mountain walls,
And like a thunderbolt he falls.

Alfred, Lord Tennyson (1809–92)

The Way Through the Woods

They shut the road through the woods
Seventy years ago.
Weather and rain have undone it again,
And now you would never know
5   There was once a road through the woods
Before they planted the trees.
It is underneath the coppice and heath
And the thin anemones.
Only the keeper sees
10   That, where the ring-dove broods,
And the badgers roll at ease,
There was once a road through the woods.

Yet, if you enter the woods
Of a summer evening late,
15   When the night-air cools on the trout-ringed pools
Where the otter whistles his mate,
(They fear not men in the woods,
Because they see so few.)
You will hear the beat of a horse's feet,
20   And the swish of a skirt in the dew,
Steadily cantering through
The misty solitudes,
As though they perfectly knew
The old lost road through the woods. . . .
25   But there is no road through the woods.

Rudyard Kipling (1865–1936)

On Wenlock Edge . . .

On Wenlock Edge the wood's in trouble;
    His forest fleece the Wrekin heaves;
The gale, it plies the saplings double,
    And thick on Severn snow the leaves.

5   'Twould blow like this through holt and hanger
    When Uricon the city stood:
'Tis the old wind in the old anger,
    But then it threshed another wood.

Then, 'twas before my time, the Roman
10   At yonder heaving hill would stare:
The blood that warms an English yeoman,
    The thoughts that hurt him, they were there.

There, like the wind through woods in riot,
    Through him the gale of life blew high;
15   The tree of man was never quiet:
    Then 'twas the Roman, now 'tis I.

The gale, it plies the saplings double,
    It blows so hard, 'twill soon be gone:
Today the Roman and his trouble
20   Are ashes under Uricon.

A. E. Housman (1859–1936)

Binsey Poplars

Felled 1879

My aspens dear, whose airy cages quelled,
Quelled or quenched in leaves the leaping sun,
All felled, felled, are all felled;
    Of a fresh and following folded rank
5   Not spared, not one
           That dandled a sandalled
        Shadow that swam or sank
On meadow and river and wind-wandering
    weed-winding bank.

10 O if we but knew what we do
        When we delve or hew –
    Hack and rack the growing green!
        Since country is so tender
To touch, her being so slender,
15 That, like this sleek and seeing ball
But a prick will make no eye at all,
    Where we, even where we mean
        To mend her we end her,
        When we hew or delve:
20 After-comers cannot guess the beauty been.
    Ten or twelve, only ten or twelve
        Strokes of havoc unselve
        The sweet especial scene,
    Rural scene, a rural scene,
25   Sweet especial rural scene.

Gerard Manley Hopkins (1844–89)

The Lake Isle of Innisfree

I will arise and go now, and go to Innisfree,
And a small cabin build there, of clay and wattles made:
Nine bean-rows will I have there, a hive for the honey-bee,
And live alone in the bee-loud glade.

5   And I shall have some peace there, for peace comes dropping slow,
Dropping from the veils of the morning to where the cricket sings;
There midnight's all a glimmer, and noon a purple glow,
And evening full of the linnet's wings.

I will arise and go now, for always night and day
10   I hear lake water lapping with low sounds by the shore;
While I stand on the roadway, or on the pavements grey,
I hear it in the deep heart's core.

William Butler Yeats (1865–1939)

Symphony in Yellow

An omnibus across the bridge
    Crawls like a yellow butterfly,
    And, here and there, a passer-by
Shows like a little restless midge.

5   Big barges full of yellow hay
    Are moored against the shadowy wharf,
    And, like a yellow silken scarf,
The thick fog hangs along the quay.

The yellow leaves begin to fade
10   And flutter from the Temple elms,
    And at my feet the pale green Thames
Lies like a rod of rippled jade.

Oscar Wilde (1854–1900)

Conveyancing

O, London is the place for all,
　　In love with loco-motion!
Still to and fro the people go
　　Like billows of the ocean;
5　Machine or man, or caravan,
　　Can all be had for paying,
When great estates, or heavy weights,
　　Or bodies want conveying.

There's always hacks about in packs,
10　　Wherein you may be shaken,
And Jarvis is not always *drunk*,
　　Tho' always *overtaken*;
In racing tricks he'll never mix,
　　His nags are in their last days,
15　And *slow* to go, altho' they show
　　As if they had their *fast days*!

Then if you like a single horse,
　　This age is quite a *cab-age*,
A car not quite so small and light
20　　As those of our Queen *Mab* age;
The horses have been *broken well*,
　　All danger is rescinded,
For some have *broken both their knees*,
　　And some are *broken winded*.

25　If you've a friend at Chelsea end,
　　The stages are worth knowing –
There is a sort, we call 'em short,
　　Although the longest going –
For some will stop at Hatchett's shop,
30　　Till you grow faint and sicky,
Perched up behind, at last to find,
　　Your dinner is all *dickey*!

Long stages run from every yard:
　　But if you're wise and frugal,
35　You'll never go with any Guard
　　That plays upon a bugle,
'Ye banks and braes,' and other lays
　　And ditties everlasting,
Like miners going all your way,
40　　With *boring* and with *blasting*.

Instead of *journeys*, people now
　　May go upon a *Gurney*,
With steam to do the horse's work,
　　By *powers of attorney*;
45　Tho' with a load it may explode,
　　And you may all be *un*-done!
And find you're going *up to Heav'n*,
　　Instead of *Up to London*!

To speak of every kind of coach,
50　　It is not my intention;
But there is still one vehicle
　　Deserves a little mention;
The world a sage has call'd a stage,
　　With all its living lumber,
55　And Malthus swears it always bears
　　Above the proper number.

The law will transfer house or land
　　For ever and a day hence,
For lighter things, watch, brooches, rings,
60　　You'll never want conveyance;
Ho! stop the thief! my handkerchief!
　　It is no sight for laughter –
Away it goes, and leaves my nose
　　To join in running after!

Thomas Hood (1799–1845)

Composed Upon Westminster Bridge, September 3, 1802

Earth has not anything to show more fair:
Dull would he be of soul who could pass by
A sight so touching in its majesty:
This City now doth, like a garment, wear
5   The beauty of the morning; silent, bare,
Ships, towers, domes, theatres, and temples lie
Open unto the fields, and to the sky;
All bright and glittering in the smokeless air.
Never did sun more beautifully steep
10   In his first splendour, valley, rock, or hill;
Ne'er saw I, never felt, a calm so deep!
The river glideth at his own sweet will:
Dear God! the very houses seem asleep;
And all that mighty heart is lying still!

William Wordsworth (1770–1850)

A Dead Harvest In Kensington Gardens

Along the graceless grass of town
They rake the rows of red and brown, –
Dead leaves, unlike the rows of hay
Delicate, touched with gold and grey,
5   Raked long ago and far away.

A narrow silence in the park,
Between the lights a narrow dark.
One street rolls on the north; and one,
Muffled, upon the south doth run;
10   Amid the mist the work is done.

A futile crop! – for it the fire
Smoulders, and, for a stack, a pyre.
So go the town's lives on the breeze,
Even as the shedding of the trees;
15   Bosom nor barn is filled with these.

Alice Meynell (1847–1922)

The Song of the Shirt

With fingers weary and worn,
    With eyelids heavy and red,
A Woman sat, in unwomanly rags,
    Plying her needle and thread –
5   Stitch! stitch! stitch!
In poverty, hunger, and dirt,
And still with a voice of dolorous pitch
She sang the 'Song of the shirt!'

    'Work! work! work!
10 While the cock is crowing aloof!
    And work – work – work,
Till the stars shine through the roof!
It's O! to be a slave
    Along with the barbarous Turk,
15 Where woman has never a soul to save,
    If this is Christian work!

    'Work – work – work
Till the brain begins to swim;
    Work – work – work
20 Till the eyes are heavy and dim!
Seam, and gusset, and band,
    Band, and gusset, and seam,
Till over the buttons I fall asleep,
    And sew them on in a dream!

25 'O! Men with Sisters dear!
    O! Men with Mothers and Wives!
It is not linen you're wearing out,
    But human creatures' lives!
    Stitch – stitch – stitch,
30   In poverty, hunger, and dirt,
Sewing at once with a double thread,
    A Shroud as well as a Shirt.

    'But why do I talk of Death?
    That Phantom of grisly bone,
35 I hardly fear his terrible shape,
    It seems so like my own –
    It seems so like my own –,
    Because of the fasts I keep,
Oh! God! that bread should be so dear,
40   And flesh and blood so cheap!

    'Work – work – work!
    My labour never flags;
And what are its wages? A bed of straw,
    A crust of bread – and rags.
45 That shatter'd roof, – and this naked floor –
    A table – a broken chair –
And a wall so blank, my shadow I thank
    For sometimes falling there!

'Work – work – work!
50   From weary chime to chime,
        Work – work – work –
    As prisoners work for crime!
        Band, and gusset, and seam,
        Seam, and gusset, and band,
55   Till the heart is sick, and the brain benumb'd,
        As well as the weary hand.

    'Work – work – work!
    In the dull December light,
        And work – work – work,
60   When the weather is warm and bright –
    While underneath the eaves
        The brooding swallows cling
    As if to show me their sunny backs
        And twit me with the spring.

65   'Oh! but to breathe the breath
    Of the cowslip and primrose sweet –
        With the sky above my head,
    And grass beneath my feet,
    For only one short hour
70   To feel as I used to feel,
    Before I knew the woes of want
        And the walk that costs a meal!

    'Oh! but for one short hour!
        A respite however brief!
75   No blessed leisure of Love or Hope,
        But only time for Grief!
    A little weeping would ease my heart,
        But in their briny bed
    My tears must stop, for every drop
80   Hinders needle and thread!'

    Seam, and gusset, and band,
    Band, and gusset, and seam,
        Work, work, work,
    Like the Engine that works by Steam!
85   A mere machine of iron and wood
        That toils for Mammon's sake –
    Without a brain to ponder and craze
        Or a heart to feel – and break!

    With fingers weary and worn,
90   With eyelids heavy and red,
    A Woman sat in unwomanly rags,
        Plying her needle and thread –
            Stitch! stitch! stitch!
        In poverty, hunger and dirt,
95   And still with a voice of dolorous pitch,
    Would that its tone could reach the Rich! –
        She sang this 'Song of the Shirt!'

Thomas Hood (1799–1845)

London

I wander through each chartered street,
Near where the chartered Thames does flow,
And mark in every face I meet
Marks of weakness, marks of woe.

5   In every cry of every man,
In every infant's cry of fear,
In every voice, in every ban,
The mind-forged manacles I hear.

How the chimney-sweeper's cry
10   Every blackening church appalls;
And the hapless soldier's sigh
Runs in blood down palace walls.

But most through midnight streets I hear
How the youthful harlot's curse
15   Blasts the newborn infant's tear,
And blights with plagues the marriage hearse.

William Blake (1757–1827)

The World

By day she woos me, soft, exceeding fair:
   But all night as the moon so changeth she;
   Loathsome and foul as hidden leprosy
And subtle serpents gliding in her hair.
5   By day she woos me to the outer air,
   Ripe fruits, sweet flowers, and full satiety:
   But through the night, a beast she grins at me,
A very monster void of love and prayer.
By day she stands a lie: by night she stands
10   In all the naked horror of the truth,
With pushing horns and clawed and clutching hands.
Is this a friend indeed, that I should sell
   My soul to her, give her my life and youth,
Till my feet, cloven too, take hold on hell?

Christina Rossetti (1830–93)

Poetry Post-1914

PART 2

Generations

SECTION E

Post-1914

For examination in June 2003, January and June 2004, January and June 2005, January 2006

You're

Clownlike, happiest on your hands,
Feet to the stars, and moon-skulled,
Gilled like a fish. A common-sense
Thumbs-down on the dodo's mode.
5   Wrapped up in yourself like a spool,
Trawling your dark as owls do.
Mute as a turnip from the Fourth
Of July to All Fools' Day,
O high-riser, my little loaf.

10   Vague as fog and looked for like mail.
Farther off than Australia.
Bent-backed Atlas, our traveled prawn.
Snug as a bud and at home
Like a sprat in a pickle jug.
15   A creel of eels, all ripples.
Jumpy as a Mexican bean.
Right, like a well-done sum.
A clean slate, with your own face on.

Sylvia Plath (1932–63)

Baby-sitting

I am sitting in a strange room listening
For the wrong baby. I don't love
This baby. She is sleeping a snuffly
Roseate, bubbling sleep; she is fair;
5   She is a perfectly acceptable child.
I am afraid of her. If she wakes
She will hate me. She will shout
Her hot midnight rage, her nose
Will stream disgustingly and the perfume
10   Of her breath will fail to enchant me.

To her I will represent absolute
Abandonment. For her it will be worse
Than for the lover cold in lonely
Sheets; worse than for the woman who waits
15   A moment to collect her dignity
Beside the bleached bone in the terminal ward.
As she rises sobbing from the monstrous land
Stretching for milk-familiar comforting,
She will find me and between us two
20   It will not come. It will not come.

Gillian Clarke (1937–)

To Edwin, at Eight Months

I thought the toughest part
would be getting limbs
to agree to government:
insurrectionary beetle,
5   you lie on your back
in a semaphore frenzy,
stunned by the uprising
in your arms and legs.
Life storms through you,
10 your eye its still centre
wonderstruck but watchful.

But when body subsided
and we sat during tea
eyeing each other solemnly
15 and mouthing our marmite
I realised my mistake:
something more awesome
is making you its own,
the mind's slow accretion.
20 All you can do is wait
quietly under your skull
for your self to arrive.

Here's your toy duck.
But since every instant
25 nudges self nearer,
maybe I should get you
your new blue truck?
A fork in your future
could this firelit evening
30 be settled by our game,
as my dangerous hands
scarper like scoutcubs
to feed your flame.

Steve Ellis (1952–   )

Growing Up

I wasn't good
At being a baby. Burrowed my way
Through the long yawn of infancy,
Masking by instinct how much I knew
5   Of the senior world, sabotaging
As far as I could, biding my time,
Biting my rattle, my brother (in private),
Shoplifting daintily into my pram.
Not a good baby,
10 No.

I wasn't good
At being a child. I missed
The innocent age. Children,
Being childish, were beneath me.
15 Adults I despised or distrusted. They
Would label my every disclosure
Precocious, naïve, whatever it was.
I disdained definition, preferred to be surly.
Not a nice child,
20 No.

I wasn't good
At adolescence. There was a dance,
A catchy rhythm; I was out of step.
My body capered, nudging me
25 With hairy, fleshy growths and monthly outbursts,
To join the party. I tried to annul
The future, pretended I knew it already,
Was caught bloody-thighed, a criminal
Guilty of puberty.
30 Not a nice girl,
No.

(My hero, intransigent Emily,
Cauterized her own-dog-mauled
Arm with a poker,
35 Struggled to die on her feet,
Never told anyone anything.)

I wasn't good
At growing up. Never learned
The natives' art of life. Conversation
40 Disintegrated as I touched it,
So I played mute, wormed along years,
Reciting the hard-learned arcane litany
Of cliché, my company passport.
Not a nice person,
45 No.

The gift remains
Masonic, dark. But age affords
A vocation even for wallflowers.
Called to be connoisseur, I collect,
50   Admire, the effortless bravura
Of other people's lives, proper and comely,
Treading the measure, shopping, chaffing,
Quarrelling, drinking, not knowing
How right they are, or how, like well-oiled bolts,
55   Swiftly and sweet, they slot into the grooves
Their ancestors smoothed out along the grain.

U. A. Fanthorpe (1929–)

To Carry the Child

To carry the child into adult life
Is good? I say it is not,
To carry the child into adult life
Is to be handicapped.

5　The child in adult life is defenceless
And if he is grown-up, knows it,
And the grown-up looks at the childish part
And despises it.

The child, too, despises the clever grown-up,
10　The man-of-the-world, the frozen,
For the child has the tears alive on his cheek
And the man has none of them.

As the child has colours, and the man sees no
Colours or anything,
15　Being easy only in things of the mind,
The child is easy in feeling.

Easy in feeling, easily excessive
And in excess powerful,
For instance, if you do not speak to the child
20　He will make trouble.

You would say a man had the upper hand
Of the child, if a child survive,
I say the child has fingers of strength
To strangle the man alive.

25　Oh it is not happy, it is never happy,
To carry the child into adulthood,
Let children lie down before full growth
And die in their infanthood

And be guilty of no man's blood.

30　But oh the poor child, the poor child, what can he do,
Trapped in a grown-up carapace,
But peer outside of his prison room
With the eye of an anarchist?

Stevie Smith (1902–71)

I Remember, I Remember

Coming up England by a different line
For once, early in the cold new year,
We stopped, and, watching men with number-plates
Sprint down the platform to familiar gates,
5   'Why, Coventry!' I exclaimed. 'I was born here.'

I leant far out, and squinnied for a sign
That this was still the town that had been 'mine'
So long, but found I wasn't even clear
Which side was which. From where those cycle-crates
10   Were standing, had we annually departed

For all those family hols? . . . A whistle went:
Things moved. I sat back, staring at my boots.
'Was that,' my friend smiled, 'where you "have your roots"?'
No, only where my childhood was unspent,
15   I wanted to retort, just where I started:

By now I've got the whole place clearly charted.
Our garden, first: where I did not invent
Blinding theologies of flowers and fruits,
And wasn't spoken to by an old hat.
20   And here we have that splendid family

I never ran to when I got depressed,
The boys all biceps and the girls all chest,
Their comic Ford, their farm where I could be
'Really myself'. I'll show you, come to that,
25   The bracken where I never trembling sat,

Determined to go through with it; where she
Lay back, and 'all became a burning mist'.
And, in those offices, my doggerel
Was not set up in blunt ten-point, nor read
30   By a distinguished cousin of the mayor,

Who didn't call and tell my father *There
Before us, had we the gift to see ahead* –
'You look as if you wished the place in Hell,'
My friend said, 'judging from your face.' 'Oh well,
35   I suppose it's not the place's fault,' I said.

'Nothing, like something, happens anywhere.'

Philip Larkin (1922–85)

Anseo

When the Master was calling the roll
At the primary school in Collegelands,
You were meant to call back *Anseo*
And raise your hand
5   As your name occurred.
Anseo, meaning here, here and now,
All present and correct,
Was the first word of Irish I spoke.
The last name on the ledger
10   Belonged to Joseph Mary Plunkett Ward
And was followed, as often as not,
By silence, knowing looks,
A nod and a wink, the Master's droll
'And where's our little Ward-of-court?'

15   I remember the first time he came back
The Master had sent him out
Along the hedges
To weigh up for himself and cut
A stick with which he would be beaten.
20   After a while, nothing was spoken;
He would arrive as a matter of course
With an ash-plant, a salley-rod.
Or, finally, the hazel-wand
He had whittled down to a whip-lash,
25   Its twist of red and yellow lacquers
Sanded and polished,
And altogether so delicately wrought
That he had engraved his initials on it.

I last met Joseph Mary Plunkett Ward
30   In a pub just over the Irish border.
He was living in the open,
In a secret camp
On the other side of the mountain.
He was fighting for Ireland,
35   Making things happen.
And he told me, Joe Ward,
Of how he had risen through the ranks
To Quartermaster, Commandant.
How every morning at parade
40   His volunteers would call back *Anseo*
And raise their hands
As their names occurred.

Paul Muldoon (1951–)

A Short Film

It was not meant to hurt.
It had been made for happy remembering
By people who were still too young
To have learned about memory.

5   Now it is a dangerous weapon, a time-bomb,
Which is a kind of body-bomb, long-term, too.
Only film, a few frames of you skipping, a few seconds,
You aged about ten there, skipping and still skipping.

Not very clear grey, made out of mist and smudge,
10   This thing has a fine fuse, less a fuse
Than a wavelength attuned, an electronic detonator
To what lies in your grave inside us.

And how that explosion would hurt
Is not just an idea of horror but a flash of fine sweat
15   Over the skin-surface, a bracing of nerves
For something that has already happened.

Ted Hughes (1930–98)

Poem

And if it snowed and snow covered the drive
he took a spade and tossed it to one side.
And always tucked his daughter up at night.
And slippered her the one time that she lied.

5   And every week he tipped up half his wage.
And what he didn't spend each week he saved.
And praised his wife for every meal she made.
And once, for laughing, punched her in the face.

And for his mum he hired a private nurse.
10   And every Sunday taxied her to church.
And he blubbed when she went from bad to worse.
And twice he lifted ten quid from her purse.

Here's how they rated him when they looked back:
sometimes he did this, sometimes he did that.

Simon Armitage (1963–   )

Follower

My father worked with a horse-plough,
His shoulders globed like a full sail strung
Between the shafts and the furrow.
The horses strained at his clicking tongue.

5   An expert. He would set the wing
And fit the bright steel-pointed sock.
The sod rolled over without breaking.
At the headrig, with a single pluck

Of reins, the sweating team turned round
10   And back into the land. His eye
Narrowed and angled at the ground,
Mapping the furrow exactly.

I stumbled in his hob-nailed wake,
Fell sometimes on the polished sod;
15   Sometimes he rode me on his back
Dipping and rising to his plod.

I wanted to grow up and plough,
To close one eye, stiffen my arm.
All I ever did was follow
20   In his broad shadow round the farm.

I was a nuisance, tripping, falling,
Yapping always. But today
It is my father who keeps stumbling
Behind me, and will not go away.

Seamus Heaney (1939–)

Imitations

In this house, in this afternoon room,
my son and I. The other side of glass
snowflakes whitewash the shed roof and the grass
this surprised April. My son is 16,
5   an approximate man. He is my chameleon,
my soft diamond, my deciduous evergreen.

Eyes half closed, he listens to pop forgeries
of music – how hard it is to know – and perhaps
dreams of some school Juliet I don't know.
10   Meanwhile, beyond the bending window,
gusting suddenly, despite a sky half blue,
a blur of white blossom, whiter snow.

And I stare, oh immortal springtime, till
I'm elsewhere and the age my cool son is,
15   my father alive again (I, his duplicate)
his high breath, my low breath, sticking to the glass
while two white butterflies stumble, held each
to each, as if by elastic, and pass.

Dannie Abse (1923–   )

from **Long Distance**

Though my mother was already two years dead
Dad kept her slippers warming by the gas,
put hot water bottles her side of the bed
and still went to renew her transport pass.

5 You couldn't just drop in. You had to phone.
He'd put you off an hour to give him time
to clear away her things and look alone
as though his still raw love were such a crime.

He couldn't risk my blight of disbelief
10 though sure that very soon he'd hear her key
scrape in the rusted lock and end his grief.
He *knew* she'd just popped out to get the tea.

I believe life ends with death, and that is all.
You haven't both gone shopping; just the same,
15 in my new black leather phone book there's your name
and the disconnected number I still call.

Tony Harrison (1937–   )

from **Long Distance**

The Flowers

After lunch my daughter picked
handfuls of the wild flowers
she knew her grandfather liked best
and piled them in the basket of her bicycle,
5   beside an empty jam-jar and a trowel;
then, swaying like a candle-bearer,
she rode off to the church
and, like a little dog, I followed her.

She cleared the grave of nettles
10   and wild parsley, and dug a shallow hole
to put the jam-jar in. She arranged
the flowers to look their best
and scraped the moss from the stone,
so you could see whose grave
15   she had been caring for.
It didn't take her long – no longer
than making his bed in the morning
when he had got too old to help her.

Not knowing how to leave him,
20   how to say goodbye, I hesitated
by the rounded grave. *Come on*,
my daughter said, *It's finished now.*
And so we got our bicycles and rode home
down the lane, moving apart
25   and coming together again,
in and out of the ruts.

Selima Hill (1945–   )

Clocks

For Cai

We walk the lanes to pick them.
'Ffwff-ffwffs'. He gives them the name
he gives to all flowers. 'Ffwff! Ffwff!'
I teach him to tell the time
5   by dandelion. 'One o'clock. Two.'
He blows me a field of gold
from the palm of his hand
and learns the power of naming.

The sun goes down in the sea
10   and the moon's translucent.
He's wary of waves and sand's
soft treachery underfoot.
'What does the sea say?' I ask.
'Ffwff! Ffwff!' he answers, then turns
15   his face to the sky and points
to the full-blown moon.

Gillian Clarke (1937–   )

The Tune the Old Cow Died Of

'The tune the old cow died of,'
My grandmother used to say
When my uncle played the flute.
She hadn't seen a cow for many a day,
5   Shut in by slate
Walls that bound her
To scullery and yard and soot-
blackened flowerpots and hart's-tongue fern.
She watched her fourteen sons grow up around her
10   In a back street,
Blocked at one end by crags of slag,
Barred at the other by the railway goods-yard gate.
The toot of the flute
Piped to a parish where never cow could earn
15   Her keep – acres of brick
With telegraph poles and chimneys reared up thick
As ricks in a harvest field.
My grandmother remembered
Another landscape where the cattle
20   Waded halfway to the knees
In swish of buttercup and yellow rattle,
And un-shorn, parasite-tormented sheep
Flopped down like grey bolsters in the shade of trees,
And the only sound
25   Was the whine of a hound
In the out-of-hunting-season summer,
Or the cheep of wide-beaked, new-hatched starlings,
Or the humdrum hum of the bees.
                                        Then
A cow meant milk, meant cheese, meant money,
30   And when a cow died
With foot-and-mouth or wandered out on the marshes
And drowned at the high tide,
The children went without whatever their father had promised.
When she was a girl
35   There was nothing funny,
My grandmother said,
About the death of a cow,
And it isn't funny now
To millions hungrier even than she was then.
40   So when the babies cried,
One after each for over fourteen years,
Or the flute squeaked at her ears,
Or the council fire-alarm let off a scream
Like steam out of a kettle and the whole mad town
45   Seemed fit to blow its lid off – she could find
No words to ease her mind
Like those remembered from her childhood fears:
'The tune the old cow died of.'

Norman Nicholson (1914–87)

West Pathway

I just hope I've the guts
to give my children
one piece of advice only:
never live
5   in a cul-de-sac.

Steve Ellis (1952–   )

The 1914–18 War (i)

Post-1914

As the Team's Head-Brass

As the team's head-brass flashed out on the turn
The lovers disappeared into the wood.
I sat among the boughs of the fallen elm
That strewed the angle of the fallow, and
5   Watched the plough narrowing a yellow square
Of charlock. Every time the horses turned
Instead of treading me down, the ploughman leaned
Upon the handles to say or ask a word,
About the weather, next about the war.
10   Scraping the share he faced towards the wood,
And screwed along the furrow till the brass flashed
Once more.
            The blizzard felled the elm whose crest
I sat in, by a woodpecker's round hole,
The ploughman said. 'When will they take it away?'
15   'When the war's over.' So the talk began –
One minute and an interval of ten,
A minute more and the same interval.
'Have you been out?' 'No.' 'And don't want to, perhaps?'
'If I could only come back again, I should.
20   I could spare an arm. I shouldn't want to lose
A leg. If I should lose my head, why, so,
I should want nothing more. . . . Have many gone
From here?' 'Yes.' 'Many lost?' 'Yes, a good few.
Only two teams work on the farm this year.
25   One of my mates is dead. The second day
In France they killed him. It was back in March,
The very night of the blizzard, too. Now if
He had stayed here we should have moved the tree.'
'And I should not have sat here. Everything
30   Would have been different. For it would have been
Another world.' 'Ay, and a better, though
If we could see all all might seem good.' Then
The lovers came out of the wood again:
The horses started and for the last time
35   I watched the clods crumble and topple over
After the ploughshare and the stumbling team.

Edward Thomas (1878–1917)

At the Movies

They swing across the screen in brave array,
    Long British columns grinding the dark grass.
Twelve months ago they marched into the grey
    Of battle; yet again behold them pass!

5   One lifts his dusty cap; his hair is bright;
    I meet his eyes, eager and young and bold.
The picture quivers into ghostly white;
    Then I remember, and my heart grows cold!

Florence Ripley Mastin (b.1896)

When you see millions of the mouthless dead . . .

When you see millions of the mouthless dead
Across your dreams in pale battalions go,
Say not soft things as other men have said,
That you'll remember. For you need not so.
5   Give them not praise. For, deaf, how should they know
It is not curses heaped on each gashed head?
Nor tears. Their blind eyes see not your tears flow.
Nor honour. It is easy to be dead.
Say only this, 'They are dead.' Then add thereto,
10   'Yet many a better one has died before.'
Then, scanning all the o'ercrowded mass, should you
Perceive one face that you loved heretofore,
It is a spook. None wears the face you knew.
Great death has made all his for evermore.

C. H. Sorley (1895–1915)

War Girls

There's the girl who clips your ticket for the train,
    And the girl who speeds the lift from floor to floor,
There's the girl who does a milk-round in the rain,
    And the girl who calls for orders at your door.
5   Strong, sensible, and fit,
            They're out to show their grit,
    And tackle jobs with energy and knack.
         No longer caged and penned up,
         They're going to keep their end up
10   Till the khaki soldier boys come marching back.

There's the motor girl who drives a heavy van,
    There's the butcher girl who brings your joint of meat,
There's the girl who cries 'All fares, please!' like a man,
    And the girl who whistles taxis up the street.
15   Beneath each uniform
           Beats a heart that's soft and warm,
    Though of canny mother-wit they show no lack;
         But a solemn statement this is,
         They've no time for love and kisses
20   Till the khaki soldier boys come marching back.

Jessie Pope (1868–1941)

In Time of War

I dreamed (God pity babes at play)
How I should love past all romance,
And how to him beloved should say,
As heroes' women say, perchance,
5 When the deep drums awake –
'Go forth: do gloriously for my dear sake.'

But now I render, blind with fear,
No lover made of dreams, but You,
O You – so commonplace, so dear,
10 So knit with all I am or do!
Now, braver thought I lack:
Only God bring you back – God bring you back!

Lesbia Thanet (dates unknown)

Of the Great White War

During the years when the white men fought each other,
I observed how the aged cried aloud in public places
Of honour and chivalry, and the duty of the young;
And how the young ceased doing the pleasant things of youth,
5   And became suddenly old,
And marched away to defend the aged.
And I observed how the aged
Became suddenly young;
And mouthed fair phrases one to the other upon the Supreme Sacrifice,
10 And turned to their account books, murmuring gravely:
Business as Usual;
And brought out the bottles of wine and drank the health
Of the young men they had sent out to die for them.

Thomas Burke (1887–1945)

Base Details

If I were fierce, and bald, and short of breath,
    I'd live with scarlet Majors at the Base,
And speed glum heroes up the line to death.
    You'd see me with my puffy petulant face,
5 Guzzling and gulping in the best hotel,
    Reading the Roll of Honour. 'Poor young chap,'
I'd say – 'I used to know his father well;
    Yes, we've lost heavily in this last scrap.'
And when the war is done and youth stone dead,
10 I'd toddle safely home and die – in bed.

Siegfried Sassoon (1886–1967)

Disabled

He sat in a wheeled chair, waiting for dark,
And shivered in his ghastly suit of grey,
Legless, sewn short at elbow. Through the park
Voices of boys rang saddening like a hymn,
5   Voices of play and pleasure after day,
Till gathering sleep had mothered them from him.

About this time Town used to swing so gay
When glow-lamps budded in the light blue trees,
And girls glanced lovelier as the air grew dim, –
10 In the old times, before he threw away his knees.
Now he will never feel again how slim
Girls' waists are, or how warm their subtle hands.
All of them touch him like some queer disease.

There was an artist silly for his face,
15 For it was younger than his youth, last year.
Now, he is old; his back will never brace;
He's lost his colour very far from here,
Poured it down shell-holes till the veins ran dry,
And half his lifetime lapsed in the hot race
20 And leap of purple spurted from his thigh.

One time he liked a blood-smear down his leg,
After the matches, carried shoulder-high.
It was after football, when he'd drunk a peg,
He thought he'd better join. – He wonders why.
25 Someone had said he'd look a god in kilts,
That's why; and maybe, too, to please his Meg,
Aye, that was it, to please the giddy jilts
He asked to join. He didn't have to beg;
Smiling they wrote his lie: aged nineteen years.
30 Germans he scarcely thought of; all their guilt,
And Austria's, did not move him. And no fears
Of Fear came yet. He thought of jewelled hilts
For daggers in plaid socks; of smart salutes;
And care of arms; and leave; and pay arrears;
35 Esprit de corps; and hints for young recruits.
And soon, he was drafted out with drums and cheers.

Some cheered him home, but not as crowds cheer Goal.
Only a solemn man who brought him fruits
Thanked him; and then enquired about his soul.

40 Now, he will spend a few sick years in institutes,
And do what things the rules consider wise,
And take whatever pity they may dole.
Tonight he noticed how the women's eyes
Passed from him to the strong men that were whole.
45 How cold and late it is! Why don't they come
And put him into bed? Why don't they come?

Wilfred Owen (1893–1918)

Sonnet

What lips my lips have kissed, and where, and why,
I have forgotten, and what arms have lain
Under my head till morning; but the rain
Is full of ghosts tonight, that tap and sigh
5   Upon the glass and listen for reply,
And in my heart there stirs a quiet pain
For unremembered lads that not again
Will turn to me at midnight with a cry.
Thus in the winter stands the lonely tree,
10   Nor knows what birds have vanished one by one,
Yet knows its boughs more silent than before:
I cannot say what loves have come and gone,
I only know that summer sang in me
A little while, that in me sings no more.

Edna St Vincent Millay (1892–1950)

The Dug-Out

Why do you lie with your legs ungainly huddled,
And one arm bent across your sullen, cold,
Exhausted face? It hurts my heart to watch you,
Deep-shadow'd from the candle's guttering gold;
5   And you wonder why I shake you by the shoulder;
Drowsy, you mumble and sigh and turn your head . . .
You are too young to fall asleep for ever;
And when you sleep you remind me of the dead.

Siegfried Sassoon (1886–1967)

Exposure

Our brains ache, in the merciless iced east winds that knive us . . .
Wearied we keep awake because the night is silent . . .
Low, drooping flares confuse our memory of the salient . . .
Worried by silence, sentries whisper, curious, nervous,
5   But nothing happens.

Watching, we hear the mad gusts tugging on the wire,
Like twitching agonies of men among its brambles.
Northward, incessantly, the flickering gunnery rumbles,
Far off, like a dull rumour of some other war.
10   What are we doing here?

The poignant misery of dawn begins to grow . . .
We only know war lasts, rain soaks, and clouds sag stormy.
Dawn massing in the east her melancholy army
Attacks once more in ranks on shivering ranks of grey,
15   But nothing happens.

Sudden successive flights of bullets streak the silence.
Less deathly than the air that shudders black with snow,
With sidelong flowing flakes that flock, pause, and renew;
We watch them wandering up and down the wind's nonchalance,
20   But nothing happens.

Pale flakes with fingering stealth come feeling for our faces –
We cringe in holes, back on forgotten dreams, and stare, snow-dazed,
Deep into grassier ditches. So we drowse, sun-dozed,
Littered with blossoms trickling where the blackbird fusses,
25   – Is it that we are dying?

Slowly our ghosts drag home: glimpsing the sunk fires, glozed
With crusted dark-red jewels; crickets jingle there;
For hours the innocent mice rejoice: the house is theirs;
Shutters and doors, all closed: on us the doors are closed, –
30   We turn back to our dying.

Since we believe not otherwise can kind fires burn;
Nor ever suns smile true on child, or field, or fruit.
For God's invincible spring our love is made afraid;
Therefore, not loath, we lie out here; therefore were born,
35   For love of God seems dying.

Tonight, this frost will fasten on this mud and us,
Shrivelling many hands, puckering foreheads crisp.
The burying-party, picks and shovels in shaking grasp,
Pause over half-known faces. All their eyes are ice,
40   But nothing happens.

Wilfred Owen (1893–1918)

Breakfast

We ate our breakfast lying on our backs,
Because the shells were screeching overhead.
I bet a rasher to a loaf of bread
That Hull United would beat Halifax
5   When Jimmy Stainthorp played full-back instead
Of Billy Bradford. Ginger raised his head
And cursed, and took the bet; and dropt back dead.
We ate our breakfast lying on our backs,
Because the shells were screeching overhead.

W. W. Gibson (1878–1962)

Returning, We Hear the Larks

Sombre the night is.
And though we have our lives, we know
What sinister threat lurks there.

Dragging these anguished limbs, we only know
5   This poison-blasted track opens on our camp –
On a little safe sleep.

But hark! joy – joy – strange joy.
Lo! heights of night ringing with unseen larks.
Music showering our upturned list'ning faces.

10   Death could drop from the dark
As easily as song –
But song only dropped,
Like a blind man's dreams on the sand
By dangerous tides,
15   Like a girl's dark hair for she dreams no ruin lies there,
Or her kisses where a serpent hides.

Isaac Rosenberg (1890–1918)

Mental Cases

Who are these? Why sit they here in twilight?
Wherefore rock they, purgatorial shadows,
Drooping tongues from jaws that slob their relish,
Baring teeth that leer like skulls' teeth wicked?
5   Stroke on stroke of pain, – but what slow panic,
Gouged these chasms round their fretted sockets?
Ever from their hair and through their hands' palms
Misery swelters. Surely we have perished
Sleeping, and walk hell; but who these hellish?

10   – These are men whose minds the Dead have ravished.
Memory fingers in their hair of murders,
Multitudinous murders they once witnessed.
Wading sloughs of flesh these helpless wander,
Treading blood from lungs that had loved laughter.
15   Always they must see these things and hear them,
Batter of guns and shatter of flying muscles,
Carnage incomparable, and human squander
Rucked too thick for these men's extrication.

Therefore still their eyeballs shrink tormented
20   Back into their brains, because on their sense
Sunlight seems a blood-smear; night comes blood-black;
Dawn breaks open like a wound that bleeds afresh.
– Thus their heads wear this hilarious, hideous,
Awful falseness of set-smiling corpses.
25   – Thus their hands are plucking at each other;
Picking at the rope-knots of their scourging;
Snatching after us who smote them, brother,
Pawing us who dealt them war and madness.

Wilfred Owen (1893–1918)

Easter Monday

(In Memoriam E.T.)

In the last letter that I had from France
You thanked me for the silver Easter egg
Which I had hidden in the box of apples
You liked to munch beyond all other fruit.
5   You found the egg the Monday before Easter,
And said, 'I will praise Easter Monday now –
It was such a lovely morning.' Then you spoke
Of the coming battle and said, 'This is the eve.
Good-bye. And may I have a letter soon.'

10   That Easter Monday was a day for praise,
It was such a lovely morning. In our garden
We sowed our earliest seeds, and in the orchard
The apple-bud was ripe. It was the eve.
There are three letters that you will not get.

Eleanor Farjeon (1881–1965)

There will come soft rains . . .

There will come soft rains and the smell of the ground,
And swallows calling with their shimmering sound;

And frogs in the pools singing at night,
And wild-plum trees in tremulous white;

5   Robins will wear their feathery fire
Whistling their whims on a low fence-wire;

And not one will know of the war, not one
Will care at last when it is done.

Not one would mind, neither bird nor tree,
10   If mankind perished utterly;

And Spring herself, when she woke at dawn,
Would scarcely know that we were gone.

Sara Teasdale (1884–1933)

How It Looks From Here

SECTION G

Post-1914

For examination in June 2006, January and June 2007, January 2008 onwards

A Consumer's Report

The name of the product I tested is *Life*,
I have completed the form you sent me
and understand that my answers are confidential.

I had it as a gift,
5   I didn't feel much while using it,
in fact I think I'd have liked to be more excited.
It seemed gentle on the hands
but left an embarrassing deposit behind.
It was not economical
10   and I have used much more than I thought
(I suppose I have about half left
but it's difficult to tell) –
although the instructions are fairly large
there are so many of them
15   I don't know which to follow, especially
as they seem to contradict each other.
I'm not sure such a thing
should be put in the way of children –
It's difficult to think of a purpose
20   for it. One of my friends says
it's just to keep its maker in a job.
Also the price is much too high.
Things are piling up so fast,
after all, the world got by
25   for a thousand million years
without this, do we need it now?
(Incidentally, please ask your man
to stop calling me 'the respondent',
I don't like the sound of it.)
30   There seems to be a lot of different labels,
sizes and colours should be uniform,
the shape is awkward, it's waterproof
but not heat resistant, it doesn't keep
yet it's very difficult to get rid of:
35   whenever they make it cheaper they seem
to put less in – if you say you don't
want it, then it's delivered anyway.
I'd agree it's a popular product,
it's got into the language; people
40   even say they're on the side of it.
Personally I think it's overdone,
a small thing people are ready
to behave badly about. I think
we should take it for granted. If its
45   experts are called philosophers or market
researchers or historians, we shouldn't
care. We are the consumers and the last
law makers. So finally, I'd buy it.
But the question of a 'best buy'
50   I'd like to leave until I get
the competitive product you said you'd send.

Peter Porter (1929–   )

Oh Grateful Colours, Bright Looks!

The grass is green
The tulip is red
A ginger cat walks over
The pink almond petals on the flower bed.
5   Enough has been said to show
It is life we are talking about. Oh
Grateful colours, bright looks! Well, to go
On. Fabricated things too – front doors and gates,
Bricks, slates, paving stones – are coloured
10 And as it has been raining and is sunny now
They shine. Only that puddle
Which, reflecting the height of the sky
Quite gives one a feeling of vertigo, shows
No colour, is a negative. Men!
15 Seize colours quick, heap them up while you can.
But perhaps it is a false tale that says
The landscape of the dead
Is colourless.

Stevie Smith (1902–71)

The Cat and the Sea

It is a matter of a black cat
On a bare cliff top in March
Whose eyes anticipate
The gorse petals;

5   The formal equation of
A domestic purr
With the cold interiors
Of the sea's mirror.

R. S. Thomas (1913–2000)

Mort aux Chats

There will be no more cats.
Cats spread infection,
cats pollute the air,
cats consume seven times
5   their own weight in food a week,
cats were worshipped in
decadent societies (Egypt
and Ancient Rome), the Greeks
had no use for cats. Cats
10   sit down to pee (our scientists
have proved it). The copulation
of cats is harrowing; they
are unbearably fond of the moon.
Perhaps they are all right in
15   their own country but their
traditions are alien to ours.
Cats smell, they can't help it,
you notice it going upstairs.
Cats watch too much television,
20   they can sleep through storms,
they stabbed us in the back
last time. There have never been
any great artists who were cats.
They don't deserve a capital C
25   except at the beginning of a sentence.
I blame my headache and my
plants dying on to cats.
Our district is full of them,
property values are falling.
30   When I dream of God I see
a Massacre of Cats. Why
should they insist on their own
language and religion, who
needs to purr to make his point?
35   Death to all cats! The Rule
of Dogs shall last a thousand years!

Peter Porter (1929–)

Rat, O Rat . . .

never in all my life have I seen
as handsome a rat as you.
Thank you for noticing my potatoes.

O Rat, I am not rich.
5   I left you a note concerning potatoes,
but I see that I placed it too high
and you could not read it.

O Rat, my wife and I are cursed
with the possession of a large and hungry dog;
10   it worries us that he might learn your name –
which is forever on our lips.

O Rat, consider my neighbour:
he has eight children (all of them older
and more intelligent than mine)
15   and if you lived in his house, Rat,

ten good Christians
(if we include his wife)
would sing your praises nightly,
whereas in my house there are only five.

Christopher Logue (1926–)

In Your Mind

The other country, is it anticipated or half-remembered?
Its language is muffled by the rain which falls all afternoon
one autumn in England, and in your mind
you put aside your work and head for the airport
5   with a credit card and a warm coat you will leave
on the plane. The past fades like newsprint in the sun.

You know people there. Their faces are photographs
on the wrong side of your eyes. A beautiful boy
in the bar on the harbour serves you a drink – what? –
10 asks you if men could possibly land on the moon.
A moon like an orange drawn by a child. No.
Never. You watch it peel itself into the sea.

Sleep. The rasp of carpentry wakes you. On the wall,
a painting lost for thirty years renders the room yours.
15 *Of course*. You go to your job, right at the old hotel, left,
then left again. You love this job. Apt sounds
mark the passing of the hours. Seagulls. Bells. A flute
practising scales. You swap a coin for a fish on the way home.

Then suddenly you are lost but not lost, dawdling
20 on the blue bridge, watching six swans vanish
under your feet. The certainty of place turns on the lights
all over town, turns up the scent on the air. For a moment
you are there, in the other country, knowing its name.
And then a desk. A newspaper. A window. English rain.

Carol Ann Duffy (1965–   )

Wedding-Wind

The wind blew all my wedding-day,
And my wedding-night was the night of the high wind;
And a stable door was banging, again and again,
That he must go and shut it, leaving me
5   Stupid in candlelight, hearing rain,
Seeing my face in the twisted candlestick,
Yet seeing nothing. When he came back
He said the horses were restless, and I was sad
That any man or beast that night should lack
10   The happiness I had.

                    Now in the day
All's ravelled under the sun by the wind's blowing.
He has gone to look at the floods, and I
Carry a chipped pail to the chicken-run,
Set it down, and stare. All is the wind
15   Hunting through clouds and forests, thrashing
My apron and the hanging cloths on the line.
Can it be borne, this bodying-forth by wind
Of joy my actions turn on, like a thread
Carrying beads? Shall I be let to sleep
20   Now this perpetual morning shares my bed?
Can even death dry up
These new delighted lakes, conclude
Our kneeling as cattle by all-generous waters?

Philip Larkin (1922–85)

Judging Distances

Not only how far away, but the way that you say it
Is very important. Perhaps you may never get
The knack of judging a distance, but at least you know
How to report on a landscape: the central sector,
5   The right of arc and that, which we had last Tuesday,
        And at least you know

That maps are of time, not place, so far as the army
Happens to be concerned – the reason being,
Is one which need not delay us. Again, you know
10   There are three kinds of tree, three only, the fir and the poplar,
And those which have bushy tops to; and lastly
        That things only seem to be things.

A barn is not called a barn, to put it more plainly,
Or a field in the distance, where sheep may be safely grazing.
15   You must never be over-sure. You must say, when reporting:
At five o'clock in the central sector is a dozen
Of what appear to be animals; whatever you do,
        Don't call the bleeders *sheep*.

I am sure that's quite clear; and suppose, for the sake of example,
20   The one at the end, asleep, endeavours to tell us
What he sees over there to the west, and how far away,
After first having come to attention. There to the west,
On the fields of summer the sun and the shadows bestow
        Vestments of purple and gold.

25   The still white dwellings are like a mirage in the heat,
And under the swaying elms a man and a woman
Lie gently together. Which is, perhaps, only to say
That there is a row of houses to the left of arc,
And that under some poplars a pair of what appear to be humans
30   Appear to be loving.

Well that, for an answer, is what we might rightly call
Moderately satisfactory only, the reason being,
Is that two things have been omitted, and those are important.
The human beings, now: in what direction are they,
35   And how far away, would you say? And do not forget
        There may be dead ground in between.

There may be dead ground in between; and I may not have got
The knack of judging a distance; I will only venture
A guess that perhaps between me and the apparent lovers,
40   (Who, incidentally, appear by now to have finished)
At seven o'clock from the houses, is roughly a distance
        Of about one year and a half.

Henry Reed (1914–86)

Mirror

I am silver and exact. I have no preconceptions.
Whatever I see I swallow immediately
Just as it is, unmisted by love or dislike.
I am not cruel, only truthful –
5   The eye of a little god, four-cornered.
Most of the time I meditate on the opposite wall.
It is pink, with speckles. I have looked at it so long
I think it is a part of my heart. But it flickers.
Faces and darkness separate us over and over.

10   Now I am a lake. A woman bends over me,
Searching my reaches for what she really is.
Then she turns to those liars, the candles or the moon.
I see her back, and reflect it faithfully.
She rewards me with tears and an agitation of hands.
15   I am important to her. She comes and goes.
Each morning it is her face that replaces the darkness.
In me she has drowned a young girl, and in me an old woman
Rises toward her day after day, like a terrible fish.

Sylvia Plath (1932–63)

Things

There are worse things than having behaved foolishly in public.
There are worse things than these miniature betrayals,
committed or endured or suspected; there are worse things
than not being able to sleep for thinking about them.
5   It is 5 a.m. All the worse things come stalking in
and stand icily about the bed looking worse and worse and worse.

Fleur Adcock (1934–   )

The Hare

Beside the river in the dead of night,
a cry, and then another, like a spell,
turns the darkened beeches into light,
the silence of the woods into a bell;
5 and in the cottage on the moonlit hill
a woman shivers in her narrow bed
to hear the hare; and then the hare is still;
she feels its dusty fur against her head,
its ginger paws, that panic like trapped flies,
10 or tiny fish that see, or sense, dry land;
she feels it move; she hears its wild cries
glittering inside her ear like sand:
he's lost inside the forest of her hair,
and finds, and steals, his mother's kisses there.

Selima Hill (1945–)

Bedfellows

An inch or so above the bed
    the yellow blindspot hovers
where the last incumbent's greasy head
    has worn away the flowers.

5 Every night I have to rest
    my head in his dead halo;
I feel his heart tick in my wrist;
    then, below the pillow,

his suffocated voice resumes
10   its dreary innuendo:
there are other ways to leave the room
    than the door and the window

Don Paterson (1963–)

Defying Gravity

Gravity is one of the oldest tricks in the book.
Let go of the book and it abseils to the ground
As if, at the centre of the earth, spins a giant yo-yo
To which everything is attached by an invisible string.

5   Tear out a page of the book and make an aeroplane.
Launch it. For an instant it seems that you have fashioned
A shape that can outwit air, that has slipped the knot.
But no. The earth turns, the winch tightens, it is wound in.

One of my closest friends is, at the time of writing,
10   Attempting to defy gravity, and will surely succeed.
Eighteen months ago he was playing rugby,
Now, seven stones lighter, his wife carries him aw-

Kwardly from room to room. Arranges him gently
Upon the sofa for the visitors. 'How are things?'
15   Asks one, not wanting to know. Pause. 'Not too bad.'
(Open brackets. Condition inoperable. Close brackets.)

Soon now, the man that I love (not the armful of bones)
Will defy gravity. Freeing himself from the tackle
He will sidestep the opposition and streak down the wing
20   Towards a dimension as yet unimagined.

Back where the strings are attached there will be a service
And homage paid to the giant yo-yo. A box of left-overs
Will be lowered into a space on loan from the clay.
Then, weighted down, the living will walk wearily away.

Roger McGough (1937–   )

I Am a Cameraman

They suffer, and I catch only the surface.
The rest is inexpressible, beyond
What can be recorded. You can't be them.
If they'd talk to you, you might guess
5   What pain is like though they might spit on you.

Film is just a reflection
Of the matchless despair of the century.
There have been twenty centuries since charity began.
Indignation is day-to-day stuff;
10   It keeps us off the streets, it keeps us watching.

Film has no words of its own.
It is a silent waste of things happening
Without us, when it is too late to help.
What of the dignity of those caught suffering?
15   It hurts me. I robbed them of privacy.

My young friends think Film will be all of Art.
It will be revolutionary proof.
Their films will not guess wrongly and will not lie.
They'll film what is happening behind barbed wire.
20   They'll always know the truth and be famous.

Politics softens everything.
Truth is known only to its victims.
All else is photographs – a documentary
The starving and the playboys perish in.
25   Life disguises itself with professionalism.

Life tells the biggest lies of all,
And draws wages from itself.
Truth is a landscape the saintly tribes live on,
And all the lenses of Japan and Germany
30   Wouldn't know how to focus on it.

Life flickers on the frame like beautiful hummingbirds.
That is the film that always comes out blank.
The painting the artist can't get shapes to fit.
The poem that shrugs off every word you try.
35   The music no one has ever heard.

Douglas Dunn (1942–)

Engineers' Corner

Why isn't there an Engineers' Corner in Westminster Abbey?
In Britain we've always made more fuss of a ballad than a blueprint
... How many schoolchildren dream of becoming great engineers?
Advertisement placed in The Times *by the Engineering Council*

We make more fuss of ballads than of blueprints –
That's why so many poets end up rich,
While engineers scrape by in cheerless garrets.
Who needs a bridge or dam? Who needs a ditch?

5   Whereas the person who can write a sonnet
Has got it made. It's always been the way,
For everybody knows that we need poems
And everybody reads them every day.

Yes, life is hard if you choose engineering –
10   You're sure to need another job as well;
You'll have to plan your projects in the evenings
Instead of going out. It must be hell.

While well-heeled poets ride around in Daimlers,
You'll burn the midnight oil to earn a crust,
15   With no hope of a statue in the Abbey,
With no hope, even, of a modest bust.

No wonder small boys dream of writing couplets
And spurn the bike, the lorry and the train.
There's far too much encouragement for poets –
20   That's why this country's going down the drain.

Wendy Cope (1945–   )

Sometimes

Sometimes things don't go, after all,
from bad to worse. Some years, muscadel
faces down frost; green thrives; the crops don't fail,
sometimes a man aims high, and all goes well.

5 A people sometimes will step back from war;
elect an honest man; decide they care
enough, that they can't leave some stranger poor.
Some men become what they were born for.

Sometimes our best efforts do not go
10 amiss; sometimes we do as we meant to.
The sun will sometimes melt a field of sorrow
that seemed hard frozen: may it happen for you.

Sheenagh Pugh (1950–   )

The 1914–18 War (ii)

SECTION H

Post-1914

For examination in June 2006, January and June 2007, January 2008 onwards

Recruiting

'Lads, you're wanted, go and help,'
On the railway carriage wall
Stuck the poster, and I thought
Of the hands that penned the call.

5   Fat civilians wishing they
'Could go and fight the Hun'.
Can't you see them thanking God
That they're over forty-one?

Girls with feathers, vulgar songs –
10 Washy verse on England's need –
God – and don't we damned well know
How the message ought to read.

'Lads, you're wanted! over there,
Shiver in the morning dew,
15 More poor devils like yourselves
Waiting to be killed by you.

Go and help to swell the names
In the casualty lists.
Help to make the column's stuff
20 For the blasted journalists.

Help to keep them nice and safe
From the wicked German foe.
Don't let him come over here!
Lads, you're wanted – out you go.'

25 There's a better word than that,
Lads, and can't you hear it come
From a million men that call
You to share their martyrdom?

Leave the harlots still to sing
30 Comic songs about the Hun,
Leave the fat old men to say
Now *we've* got them on the run.

Better twenty honest years
Than their dull three score and ten.
35 Lads, you're wanted. Come and learn
To live and die with honest men.

You shall learn what men can do
If you will but pay the price,
Learn the gaiety and strength
40 In the gallant sacrifice.

Take your risk of life and death
Underneath the open sky.
Live clean or go out quick –
Lads, you're wanted. Come and die.

E. A. Mackintosh (1893–1917)

Joining the Colours

(West Kents, Dublin, August 1914)

There they go marching all in step so gay!
    Smooth-cheeked and golden, food for shells and guns.
Blithely they go as to a wedding day,
        The mothers' sons.

5   The drab street stares to see them row on row
    On the high tram-tops, singing like the lark.
Too careless-gay for courage, singing they go
        Into the dark.

With tin whistles, mouth-organs, any noise,
10   They pipe the way to glory and the grave;
Foolish and young, the gay and golden boys
        Love cannot save.

High heart! High courage! The poor girls they kissed
    Run with them: they shall kiss no more, alas!
15 Out of the mist they stepped – into the mist
        Singing they pass.

Katherine Tynan Hinkson (1861–1931)

The Target

I shot him, and it had to be
One of us! 'Twas him or me.
'Couldn't be helped,' and none can blame
Me, for you would do the same.

5   My mother, she can't sleep for fear
Of what might be a-happening here
To me. Perhaps it might be best
To die, and set her fears at rest.

For worst is worst, and worry's done.
10 Perhaps he was the only son . . .
Yet God keeps still, and does not say
A word of guidance any way.

Well, if they get me, first I'll find
That boy, and tell him all my mind,
15 And see who felt the bullet worst,
And ask his pardon, if I durst.

All's tangle. Here's my job.
A man might rave, or shout, or sob;
And God He takes no sort of heed.
20 This is a bloody mess indeed.

Ivor Gurney (1890–1937)

The Send-Off

Down the close darkening lanes they sang their way
To the siding-shed,
And lined the train with faces grimly gay.

Their breasts were stuck all white with wreath and spray
5   As men's are, dead.

Dull porters watched them, and a casual tramp
Stood staring hard,
Sorry to miss them from the upland camp.

Then, unmoved, signals nodded, and a lamp
10   Winked to the guard.

So secretly, like wrongs hushed-up, they went.
They were not ours:
We never heard to which front these were sent;

Nor there if they yet mock what women meant
15   Who gave them flowers.

Shall they return to beating of great bells
In wild train-loads?
A few, a few, too few for drums and yells,

May creep back, silent, to village wells,
20   Up half-known roads.

Wilfred Owen (1893–1918)

Spring Offensive

Halted against the shade of a last hill
They fed, and eased of pack-loads, were at ease;
And leaning on the nearest chest or knees
Carelessly slept.
     But many there stood still
5 To face the stark blank sky beyond the ridge,
Knowing their feet had come to the end of the world.
Marvelling they stood, and watched the long grass swirled
By the May breeze, murmurous with wasp and midge;
And though the summer oozed into their veins
10 Like an injected drug for their bodies' pains,
Sharp on their souls hung the imminent ridge of grass,
Fearfully flashed the sky's mysterious glass.

Hour after hour they ponder the warm field
And the far valley behind, where buttercups
15 Had blessed with gold their slow boots coming up;
When even the little brambles would not yield
But clutched and clung to them like sorrowing arms.
They breathe like trees unstirred.

Till like a cold gust thrills the little word
20 At which each body and its soul begird
And tighten them for battle. No alarms
Of bugles, no high flags, no clamorous haste, –
Only a lift and flare of eyes that faced
The sun, like a friend with whom their love is done.
25 O larger shone that smile against the sun, –
Mightier than his whose bounty these have spurned.

So, soon they topped the hill, and raced together
Over an open stretch of herb and heather
Exposed. And instantly the whole sky burned
30 With fury against them; earth set sudden cups
In thousands for their blood; and the green slope
Chasmed and deepened sheer to infinite space.

Of them who running on that last high place
Breasted the surf of bullets, or went up
35 On the hot blast and fury of hell's upsurge,
Or plunged and fell away past this world's verge,
Some say God caught them even before they fell.

But what say such as from existence' brink
Ventured but drave too swift to sink,
40 The few who rushed in the body to enter hell,
And there out-fiending all its fiends and flames
With superhuman inhumanities,
Long-famous glories, immemorial shames –
And crawling slowly back, have by degrees
45 Regained cool peaceful air in wonder –
Why speak not they of comrades that went under?

Wilfred Owen (1893–1918)

The Bohemians

Certain people would not clean their buttons,
Nor polish buckles after latest fashions,
Preferred their hair long, putties comfortable,
Barely escaping hanging, indeed hardly able,
5   In Bridge and smoking without army cautions
Spending hours that sped like evil for quickness,
(While others burnished brasses, earned promotions)
These were those ones who jested in the trench,
While others argued of army ways, and wrenched
10 What little soul they had still further from shape,
And died off one by one, or became officers
Without the first of dream, the ghost of notions
Of ever becoming soldiers, or smart and neat,
Surprised as ever to find the army capable
15 Of sounding 'Lights out' to break a game of Bridge,
As to fear candles would set a barn alight.
In Artois or Picardy they lie – free of useless fashions.

Ivor Gurney (1890–1937)

Lamentations

I found him in the guard-room at the Base.
From the blind darkness I had heard his crying
And blundered in. With puzzled, patient face
A sergeant watched him; it was no good trying
5   To stop it; for he howled and beat his chest.
And, all because his brother had gone west,
Raved at the bleeding war; his rampant grief
Moaned, shouted, sobbed, and choked, while he was kneeling
Half-naked on the floor. In my belief
10 Such men have lost all patriotic feeling.

Siegfried Sassoon (1886–1967)

The Deserter

There was a man, – don't mind his name,
Whom Fear had dogged by night and day.
He could not face the German guns
And so he turned and ran away.
5   Just that – he turned and ran away,
But who can judge him, you or I?
God makes a man of flesh and blood
Who yearns to live and not to die.
And this man when he feared to die
10 Was scared as any frightened child,
His knees were shaking under him,
His breath came fast, his eyes were wild.
I've seen a hare with eyes as wild,
With throbbing heart and sobbing breath.
15 But oh! it shames one's soul to see
A man in abject fear of death.
But fear had gripped him, so had death;
His number had gone up that day,
They might not heed his frightened eyes,
20 They shot him when the dawn was grey.
Blindfolded, when the dawn was grey,
He stood there in a place apart,
The shots rang out and down he fell,
An English bullet in his heart.
25 An English bullet in his heart!
But here's the irony of life, –
His mother thinks he fought and fell
A hero, foremost in the strife.
So she goes proudly; to the strife
30 Her best, her hero son she gave.
O well for her she does not know
He lies in a deserter's grave.

Winifred M. Letts (1887–1972)

The Hero

'Jack fell as he'd have wished,' the Mother said,
And folded up the letter that she'd read.
'The Colonel writes so nicely.' Something broke
In the tired voice that quavered to a choke.
5 She half looked up. 'We mothers are so proud
Of our dead soldiers.' Then her face was bowed.

Quietly the Brother Officer went out.
He'd told the poor old dear some gallant lies
That she would nourish all her days, no doubt.
10 For while he coughed and mumbled, her weak eyes
Had shone with gentle triumph, brimmed with joy,
Because he'd been so brave, her glorious boy.

He thought how 'Jack', cold-footed, useless swine,
Had panicked down the trench that night the mine
15 Went up at Wicked Corner; how he'd tried
To get sent home, and how, at last, he died,
Blown to small bits. And no one seemed to care
Except that lonely woman with white hair.

Siegfried Sassoon (1886–1967)

The Falling Leaves

November 1915

Today, as I rode by,
I saw the brown leaves dropping from their tree
In a still afternoon,
When no wind whirled them whistling to the sky,
5 But thickly, silently,
They fell, like snowflakes wiping out the noon;
And wandered slowly thence
For thinking of a gallant multitude
Which now all withering lay,
10 Slain by no wind of age or pestilence,
But in their beauty strewed
Like snowflakes falling on the Flemish clay.

Margaret Postgate Cole (1893–1980)

In Flanders Fields

In Flanders fields the poppies blow
Between the crosses, row on row
    That mark our place; and in the sky
    The larks, still bravely singing, fly
5 Scarce heard amid the guns below.

We are the Dead. Short days ago
We lived, felt dawn, saw sunset glow,
    Loved and were loved, and now we lie
    In Flanders fields.

10 Take up our quarrel with the foe:
To you from failing hands we throw
    The torch; be yours to hold it high.
    If ye break faith with us who die
We shall not sleep, though poppies grow
15   In Flanders fields.

John McCrae (1872–1918)

The Seed-Merchant's Son

The Seed-Merchant has lost his son,
His dear, his loved, his only one.

So young he was. Even now it seems
He was a child with a child's dreams.

5   He would race over the meadow-bed
With his bright, bright eyes and his cheeks all red.

Fair and healthy and long of limb:
It made one young just to look at him.

His school books, into the cupboard thrust,
10   Have scarcely had time to gather dust.

Died in the war . . . And it seems his eyes
Must have looked at death with a child's surprise.

The Seed-Merchant goes on his way:
I saw him out on his land today;

15   Old to have fathered so young a son,
And now the last glint of his youth is gone.

What could one say to him in his need?
Little there seemed to say indeed.

So still he was that the birds flew round
20   The grey of his head without a sound,

Careless and tranquil in the air,
As if naught human were standing there.

. . .

Oh, never a soul could understand
Why he looked at the earth, and the seed in his hand,

25   As he had never before seen seed or sod:
I heard him murmur: 'Thank God, thank God!'

Agnes Grozier Herbertson (dates unknown)

The Parable of the Old Man and the Young

So Abram rose, and clave the wood, and went,
And took the fire with him, and a knife.
And as they sojourned both of them together,
Isaac the first-born spake and said, My Father,
5 Behold the preparations, fire and iron,
But where the lamb, for this burnt-offering?
Then Abram bound the youth with belts and straps,
And builded parapets and trenches there,
And stretchèd forth the knife to slay his son.
10 When lo! an Angel called him out of heaven,
Saying, Lay not thy hand upon the lad,
Neither do anything to him, thy son.
Behold! Caught in a thicket by its horns,
A Ram. Offer the Ram of Pride instead.

15 But the old man would not so, but slew his son,
And half the seed of Europe, one by one.

Wilfred Owen (1893–1918)

Spring in War-Time

Now the sprinkled blackthorn snow
    Lies along the lovers' lane
Where last year we used to go –
    Where we shall not go again.

5   In the hedge the buds are new,
    By our wood the violets peer –
Just like last year's violets, too,
    But they have no scent this year.

Every bird has heart to sing
10   Of its nest, warmed by its breast;
We had heart to sing last spring,
    But we never built our nest.

Presently red roses blown
    Will make all the garden gay . . .
15 Not yet have the daisies grown
    On your clay.

Edith Nesbit (1858–1924)

Perhaps –

(To R. A. L. Died of Wounds in France, December 23rd, 1915)

Perhaps some day the sun will shine again,
    And I shall see that still the skies are blue,
And feel once more I do not live in vain,
    Although bereft of You.

5   Perhaps the golden meadows at my feet
    Will make the sunny hours of Spring seem gay,
And I shall find the white May blossoms sweet,
    Though You have passed away.

Perhaps the summer woods will shimmer bright,
10   And crimson roses once again be fair,
And autumn harvest fields a rich delight,
    Although You are not there.

Perhaps some day I shall not shrink in pain
    To see the passing of the dying year,
15 And listen to the Christmas songs again,
    Although You cannot hear.

But, though kind Time may many joys renew,
    There is one greatest joy I shall not know
Again, because my heart for loss of You
20   Was broken, long ago.

Vera Brittain (1893–1970)

Reported Missing

My thought shall never be that you are dead:
Who laughed so lately in this quiet place.
The dear and deep-eyed humour of that face
Held something ever living, in Death's stead.
5   Scornful I hear the flat things they have said
And all their piteous platitudes of pain.
I laugh! I laugh! – For you will come again –
This heart would never beat if you were dead.
The world's adrowse in twilight hushfulness,
10 There's purple lilac in your little room,
And somewhere out beyond the evening gloom
Small boys are culling summer watercress.
Of these familiar things I have no dread
Being so very sure you are not dead.

Anna Gordon Keown (1899–1957)